Move the Rock of Academic Writing

A complete manual on the academic writing process for beginners and intermediate students

By EssayShark

Copyright Page

Table of Contents

Acknowledgments Page

We are proud to see our book published. Listed below are the people to whom we are much obliged. They helped us to write, edit, and prepare the book for publication. Due to their creativeness, persistence, personal involvement, and talent, our book was able to be released. All those people whose names are listed below are great experts in their fields, and our company is very lucky to work with such talents. The close and sufficient collaboration of our editors, publishers, designers, and, of course, writer lead to the result that you can appraise now. Meet our team:

Project editor: Derek Lynch

Guide author: Ulyana Sokolova

Publisher: Matthew Wright

Production editor: Edward Mills

Focus group: Justin Gray, Melanie Price, Eva Foster, Brooke Woods

Cover page: Amanda Scott

Proofreader: Trenton Campbell

Editorial assistant: Paul Hunt

Concept by: Alan Bennet

Introduction

This book is for those who are tired of gathering small pieces of useful information about writing academic papers or essays from dozens of sources. This book is for students who are currently studying in educational affiliations and feel as though they are "dummies" when it comes to academic writing. This book is also for those who are going to walk the path of a scholar in the future. Sounds like this book is for you, doesn't it?

With our book, you will no longer need to look for information on writing which is chaotically scattered on the internet—we have stored all necessary data in one handbook. In *Move the Rock of Academic Writing*, you'll find practical tips and recommendations on writing various academic papers and essays, in particular. You will know how to format your paper in MLA, APA, Chicago, and Harvard style. You will have the ability to pick up scholarly phrases from the "Academic Phrase Book" section. In addition, you will practice writing using the guidelines of *Move the Rock of Academic Writing*.

Move the Rock of Academic Writing was designed according to our experience of working with students for many years. It is not the book that you read and leave to collect dust on the shelf. It is the one you would like to keep near your place of study at all times. Now, it's time to absorb the standards of academic writing, so move further, dear reader!

Chapter 1. The Purpose of Academic Writing

Academic writing is a type of written narration that is accepted in educational and scholarly fields. It helps students and scholars to share their opinions concerning different scientific issues. Academic writing has a strong set of rules that differentiates it from other written styles.

In this chapter of our guide you will learn about:

- The main features of academic writing and its purpose.
- Differences between academic and non-academic writing styles.
- The importance of good academic writing skills.
- The significance of critical thinking.
- Types of academic papers.
- Helpful tips for different kinds of academic papers.
- Diverse style characteristics that appeal to academic narration in general and each type of essay in particular.
- Peculiarities of active and passive voice that are used for narration.
- Mistakes that are common.
- Supporting ideas that make sentences logically connected.

You will find out why:

- The style of academic writing is concise and clear.
- Academic writing is structured.
- Scholarly essays answer the specific questions that were set.
- Scholarly essays are made with a reference to opinions of other experts in a chosen field.
- Academic works allow students to demonstrate their personal understanding of a subject through a precise analysis of other scientific writings.
- Language units and tenses are relevant to the meaning and purpose of writing.
- Academic works are always objective.

After studying this chapter, you will be able to develop scholarly papers correctly according to the main function of academic writing, which is to tell about a complicated subject in a way that representatives of the general public can easily understand it.

Our guide will give the most important tips and examples for you to create successful academic works and improve your school achievements.

1.1. The Features of Academic Writing

Academic writing is accepted as the main method for written communication in the scientific field. With the help of this method, scholars can describe complex ideas and concepts in a clear way. Academic writing has strong features that remain stable in all forms of written samples. Therefore, it serves as a conventional method of speaking among languages of medicine, law, economics, and other scholarly branches. Students refer to the academic style when preparing writing assignments for school subjects. This partly-scientific work allows them to learn more about a topic, create a personal opinion, and express it in a scholarly way. Well-written academic papers are an integral part of successful progress in higher education.

The main purpose of academic writing is to explain complex issues to a wide audience so that the information conveyed will be as clear as possible to representatives of all professions.

The main features of academic writing are:

- **Third-person exposition.** In academic writing, narratives are described mostly through the third-person perspective rather than through the first-person perspective.

  First-person narrative: *My analysis of the latest studies shows that air pollution can be prevented by the common usage of electric cars.*

  Third-person narrative: *According to the latest studies, air pollution can be prevented by the common usage of electric cars.*

- **Particular structural elements.** The goal of academic writing is to show a fresh approach to a problem of interest. Each sample has to contain a *thesis statement* which defines an opinion that will be proved in the paper.

<u>A good (debatable) thesis statement</u>: *Although authorities spend 30 percent of the budget on limiting pollution, 15 percent has to be directed to the incorporation of electric cars.* In order to create a good problem definition, a writer has to develop his personal view of the issue but place it in correlation with the perspectives of others. For this reason, works that were studied during the research have to be presented in a *list of references* at the end of the paper. *Footnotes* and *endnotes* can also be used for this purpose.

- **Formal language.** There are certain words, word forms, and phrases that are not acceptable in academic writing due to their colloquial nature (*first-person pronouns*: I, we, me, us; *contractions*: can't, aren't, wouldn't; *abbreviations and short forms of words*: TV, photo).

- **Terse style.** Facts that are stated in academic papers should not be overloaded with too many words while being described. It is necessary to use the most appropriate terms and make statements as precise as possible. At the same time, sentences should not be short or simple.

    <u>A wordy sentence</u>: *After many years of examination, researchers arrived at the conclusion that the problem of air pollution has a negative impact on the entirety of planet Earth.*

    <u>A concise sentence</u>: *Researchers concluded air pollution to be a problem with a global reach.*

- **Objectiveness.** Alongside formal language, observations should be objective. Reference arguments help to achieve impartiality. Therefore, the outlook made in the thesis statement should be described from different points of view and also with contrasting examples.

- **Arguments based on evidence.** Each argument of the writing has to be based on facts from credible scholarly sources.

- **Complex understanding of the problem.** While making a paper in an academic style, the writer should see the whole picture of his work in order to make the description consistent and address all arguments.

- **Accurate grammar skills.** Academic writing requires sufficient knowledge of the language used, including rules of grammar and word spelling.

Differences of Academic and Non-Academic Writing

In order to understand how features of academic writing work in practice, it is helpful to compare them with specific characteristics of non-academic writing. For the comparison, see the table below.

Academic Writing	Non-Academic Writing
Introduction is logically organized with a thesis statement as the last sentence.	A short introductory paragraph is included.
Each paragraph of the main body begins with an introductory sentence that contains one argument. The rest of the paragraph supports it. Each paragraph depicts a separate argument.	Paragraphs of the main body might not be congruent with each other. Each paragraph might present another issue of the writing. This shows a narrative instead of the proving nature of the work.
All arguments are supported by facts from credible sources.	Arguments do not need to be supported by other sources. They might be based on a personal view of the writer.
Ideas from credible sources are incorporated in the paper. They are presented by direct quotations (marked with quotation marks "") or by indirect quotations (paraphrasing).	It is not necessary to incorporate outside ideas into the writing. If they are present, they are often written as direct quotations.
Personal statements such as "I think" and "to my mind" are omitted.	The opinion of the writer is stated through personal statements that refer to the writer.
Formal words are used (terminate, definitely, completely, equivalent) with a subject-specific vocabulary (appropriate, concerns, consequences, impact).	Words from a colloquial style, such as metaphors, phrasal verbs, and tropes are used.
A conclusion that summarizes findings in the paper is established.	Personal experiences and stories are incorporated.

Importance of Academic Writing Skills

In order to understand the importance of good academic writing skills, it is significant to see and understand the advantages. More specifically, having good academic writing skills allows the writer to:

- Understand and analyze scientific data.

- Develop an ability to create a debatable thesis statement based on studied information.

- Construct valid arguments grounded in learned facts to support a thesis statement.

- Understand proper methods of reasoning.

- Learn how to make consistent writing.

- Apply knowledge and creative skills in a chosen field for the personal comprehension of a problem.

- Expand attainments through scientific research.

- Receive high grades in study.

- Enter a scientific society.

Works Cited

AQA Realising potential. "Subject-Specific Vocabulary." *aqa.org.uk,*
    www.aqa.org.uk/resources/geography/as-and-a-level/geography/teach/subject-specific-
    vocabulary. Accessed 8 July 2017.

British Council. "Importance of Academic Writing Skills at the University." *britishcouncil.id,*
    webcache.googleusercontent.com. Accessed 8 July 2017.

Rambo, Randy. "English Composition. Formal Writing Voice." *ivcc.edu,*
    www2.ivcc.edu/rambo/tip_formal_writing_voice.htm. Accessed 8 July 2017.

The Purdue Online Writing Lab. "Academic Writing." *purdue.edu,*
    owl.english.purdue.edu/owl/section/1/2/. Accessed 8 July 2017.

Uni Learning. "Academic Writing. Formal Language." *uow.edu.au,*
    unilearning.uow.edu.au/academic/2bi.html. Accessed 8 July 2017.

Uni Learning. "Academic Writing. Language to Avoid." *uow.edu.au,*
    unilearning.uow.edu.au/academic/2e.html. Accessed 8 July 2017.

USC Libraries. "Organizing Your Social Sciences Research Paper: Academic Writing Style."
    usc.edu, libguides.usc.edu/writingguide/academicwriting. Accessed 8 July 2017.

1.2. Types of Academic Papers

There are four major types of academic writing:

- Analytical.

- Critical.

- Persuasive.

- Descriptive.

In most academic papers they are all combined. For example, in order to make an adequate research paper concerning any scientific subject, is it necessary to:

- Critically review previously made studies regarding a point of interest in order to find out examinational opportunities.

- Descriptively summarize methods used for information collection.

- Descriptively and analytically present data which resulted from the experiment or analysis.

- Analytically state the discussion section where findings are again compared to research questions.

- Persuasively describe findings and their interpretations.

Four mentioned types of academic writing are implemented through different kinds of academic papers. The most common of them boil down to the following writings.

Essay

- Essays are used to answer questions, confirm an argument, and state a subjective opinion on a particular topic with a reference to supportive evidence.

- Except for personal essays, the majority of them include a thesis statement which is proved throughout the whole work.

- The average length of an essay varies from 300 to 5000 words.

- Essays have peculiar types and can be admission, argumentative, comparison, descriptive, cause and effect, expository, or personal essays.

Research Paper

- Research papers give detailed information about a particular subject based on research conducted.

- It is usually longer than an essay.

- Research papers always include a thesis statement.

- A literature review may be included, where previously made studies concerning the subject are analyzed.

Book Review

- Usually, a book review serves as an assignment for students who study literature.

- It consists of reading and stating a personal opinion on the material.

- Such type moves beyond books and can be used, for example, for a movie review.

Article

- Articles can be made as an analysis of previously made research.

- This format may be addressed to a particular audience.

- Articles can be aimed at proving a statement.

Dissertation Proposal

- A dissertation proposal is represented as a big research project of which the goal is to give a solution to a particular scientific problem with a uniqueness inclusion.

- This work can be completed only after permission to research the potential concept is approved.

Report

- A report includes the studying of a particular material and its written formal analysis in the form of a presentation.
- A report may show a final result of a study.

Reflective Writing

- Reflective writing is usually made after a particular subject has been studied for a certain period.
- The aim is to show the ability of students to draw conclusions from covered information and evaluate personal progress.
- It helps to clarify learned facts and develop an individual understanding.
- Reflective writing is written in a more informal style than traditional academic writing.
- This style may take the form of blog posts or journal entries.
- Reflective writing can later be included in essays and reports.

Tips to Remember about Academic Papers

No matter which type of academic paper is used, there are several features that are peculiar to all of them:

- Every academic paper is linear. It is based on one central point that is proved in each part of the work. All paragraphs support the main argument.
- All academic papers are objective, complex, and formal. They are always made according to a strong plan which is made with an aim to cover all important issues of research.
- Objectiveness means that the manner of writing is impersonal. In this way, the author focuses on information itself instead of his personality and interpretation.
- Accuracy and responsibility of supportive data is a key. It is important to understand contextual studies of a chosen field, see perspectives for further research, and carefully interpret findings.

Writing Style Characteristics

An academic style paper has special writing aspects which have to be considered.

Precision. Academic papers usually include figures and facts that have to be stated precisely.

Complexity. The language of academic papers is more complex than its spoken variant. It includes specific vocabulary, longer words, passives, subordinate clauses, and noun-based instead of verb-based phrases. Despite the fact that academic writing is concise, it is normally packed with complex sentences and grammatical constructions.

Formality. It is not appropriate to use colloquial expressions and words in academic writing.

Distinctiveness. Every paragraph of an academic paper refers to the overall thesis statement or main idea of the work. The author has to unite all parts of the paper, demonstrating links and transitions of thought between them.

Academic writing is a complex topic which covers types of written samples and rules related to their composition. Appropriate knowledge in this area allows students to widen their writing abilities and complete writing assignments of different kinds and levels of complexity.

Works Cited

Gillett, Andy. "Academic Writing: Features of Academic Writing." *uefap.com*, www.uefap.com/writing/feature/featfram.htm. Accessed 7 August. 2017.

North Bend Library. "Academic Writing Tutorial: Common Types of Papers." *northbendlibrary.com*, www.northbendlibrary.com/the-difference-between-different-types-of-academic-writing.php. Accessed 7 August. 2017.

The University of Melbourne. "Reflective Writing." *unimelb.edu.au*, airport.unimelb.edu.au/gate2/writing/types/reflective/. Accessed 7 August. 2017.

The University of Sydney. "Types of Academic Writing." *sydney.edu.au*, sydney.edu.au/students/writing/types-of-academic-writing.html. Accessed 7 August. 2017.

1.3. Active and Passive Voice in Academic Writing

As was discussed before, academic writing implies an objective presentation of information. In order to make statements as impersonal as possible, writers refer to the usage of the passive voice. It helps to direct the reader's attention to an outlined material rather than to the writer's personality.

Active or Passive Voice?

The main reason for the usage of passive voice boils down to the fact that it directs focus on the subjects which experience the action described. In such a way, the cause of the action appears to be invisible. Compare:

Passive: *The initial study <u>was made</u> in a draft form in 2005, and in 2016 it <u>was subjected</u> to significant changes.*

Active: *I <u>made</u> a draft of the initial study in 2005 and in 2016 I <u>was finally able</u> to add significant changes.*

In the first example, the main focus is on the study and its development through time. Readers understand the difference between the two variants of the research. The writer prepares them for further discussion concerning the last version with significant changes.

In the second example, the central focus is on the writer, who wrote the draft of the study and then waited 11 years to make a final version. In this construction, readers may focus on the problems that the writer could face instead of focusing on the research itself.

15

Why Active Voice Is Important

Passive voice is not always the best choice. It can not fully replace active voice since it is also important for readers to have an idea of the agents and sources of events and issues in academic papers.

When a text is fully written in the passive voice, it is easy for the reader to lose the agents of the described actions, so the writing appears to be packed with concepts and issues instead of people. A certain level of activeness in research writing is allowed, and needed for clarity.

Advantages of Active Voice

Consequently, active voice gives authorship to the author of the writing. It is highly recommended to use it in a discussion section of a research paper. As was stated before, in this part of an academic work, the writer makes conclusions concerning his study and proposes ideas for further investigation. In order to highlight his personal impact on a research topic, a certain amount of authorial identification is necessary. That is why active voice works better in the discussion section. In addition to this, it is also beneficial to use it when the methods of research are discussed. Despite the academism of investigative techniques, each expert chooses those that satisfy personal needs and serve the purpose as best as possible.

When to Use Active Voice

Active voice is used in a number of ways:
- **During the discussion section of the paper.** *<u>Our research has shown</u> that despite the fact that disabled people face many social problems, it is not right to separate them from society by putting them into special places with fewer obstacles. It is better to change the environment than to make a social gap.* (The author marks his findings to contradistinguish them with conclusions previously made by other experts.)
- **In the methods of research section.** *<u>An interprofessional group of researchers used</u> a sampling method of the study which boils down to a creation of a systematic table that includes information about all patients and their diagnoses. <u>Medical workers observed</u> participants seven times. <u>They developed</u> cause and effect relations which led to the infection.* (The author indicates that the study was conducted by specialists from different medical fields who chose a particular way to investigate patients.)

- **In general when it is necessary to emphasize the "doer" of the action.** _Society did not approve his innovations and estimated him as an eccentric. Such a reputation was held for the next two centuries. Nevertheless, the opponents were aggressive and jealous, and the scientist hid his findings in Tibet._

In such a way, it turns out that the active voice is important for talking about those who participate in the scientific process.

Passive Voice

Conversely, passive voice focuses on what was done to the subject. When it comes to sentence structure, it appears that the subject which performs the action comes after the action itself (_verb_).

Passive: _The Pacific ocean was stirred up by many talented surfers at the US Open of Surfing competition._ (Despite the fact that here the subject stays before the predicate, the cause of the action goes after the description of the action.)

Active: _Many talented surfers stirred up the Pacific ocean at the US Open of Surfing competition._ (The cause of the action goes before the description of the action.)

When to Use Passive Voice

Passive voice is used when:

- It is irrelevant to name the doer of the action again. It was stated previously and now seems to be obvious.

    The control group consisted of five-year-old kids of both genders. Written permissions for the trial were signed by all parents. (The passive allows to omit the words "of the kids.")

    The results were found and the conclusions were made. (The passive voice allows "by us" to be omitted.)

- The doer can be interpreted differently (who or what is not important).

    In the medieval period, a physical beauty was estimated as a great curse and was thought to be an act of the Devil. (It does not matter who in particular conceived physical beauty as a damnation; it could be society, authorities, or religious personages.)

- The doer is unknown.

The ancient paintings were found around the middle of the tenth century. (We do not know who exactly found them.)

The question was asked a long time ago. (It is not known who first did this.)

- The question is about a general truth, or a well-known issue.

    Social prejudices are created to be found ridiculous lately. (This is by anyone or anything.)

- It has to be an emphasis on a thing upon which actions were taken.

    Although Chromium can be found in different foods, there are some of them which are the richest.

- It is also possible to use passive voice in the methods section of the paper.

    According to a great number of participants, a type of research was determined as quantitative. Respondents were selected randomly.

When to Avoid Passive Voice

Sometimes passive voice only disturbs the sequence and clearness of a discussion. Pay attention to the following issues:

- Too many passive sentences in a row makes the cause of the actions unclear:

    The question <u>appeared to be interesting</u> both to physicists and astronomers. It <u>was taken</u> on a case right away. (It is not clear who actually took it: physicists, astronomers, or researchers from both these fields.)

- The main purpose of academic writing is to discuss a particular subject from a new point of view. That is why differences between previously made conclusions and present ideas need to be made in a clear way. Passive constructions do not allow to name those who make current research:

    In order to develop a better understanding of a subject, a new theory <u>was proposed</u>. (By whom? The present author, the previous researcher, or by a professor who gave an assignment?)

- Sometimes students use passive voice in order to hide gaps in their knowledge.

    The Internet was created towards the end of the twentieth century. (By whom it was created?)

- Passive sentences are usually wordy, long, and indirect, with complicated constructions. That is why they are rather difficult for reading. Consequently, they can be used to make larger papers. Compare two sentences about one event that is described in active and passive voices:

> **Passive:** *Since the agreement <u>was signed</u> by Mr. Taylor right before the explosion happened and his body was found with three gunshot wounds, his whole company <u>had to be questioned</u> about their involvement in the case.*

> **Active:** *Mr. Taylor <u>signed the agreement</u> and the <u>explosion happened</u> right away. His body was found with three gunshot wounds. It is quite possible that <u>his company is involved</u> in the case.* (There are two sentences, and they are easier for reading than the previous longer one.)

Further Suggestions for Using Passive and Active Voices

All in all, there has to be a certain balance between active and passive constructions in academic papers. Despite the fact that active sentences seem to be very simple and highly personal, they are necessary for academic writing. They help to make scientific works concise so the readers can easily ascertain the information provided. What is more, every research paper should be made with an intention to bring out new dimensions of the subject. At that rate, it is beneficial for authors to confirm their authorship in the case of mixing their ideas with others', which can be estimated as plagiarism.

A careful and moderate use of active and passive voices makes academic writing clear, scientific, and pleasant for reading.

Works Cited

Monarch University. "Active or Passive Voice?" *monash.edu.au*,

www.monash.edu.au/lls/llonline/writing/general/lit-reviews/5.xml. Accessed 10 August 2017.

Toadvine, April, Brizee, Allen, and Angeli, Elizabeth. "Active and Passive Voice." *purdue.edu*,

owl.english.purdue.edu/owl/owlprint/539/. Accessed 10 August 2017.

The Writing Center. "Use the Active Voice." *wisc.edu*,

writing.wisc.edu/Handbook/CCS_activevoice.html. Accessed 10 August 2017.

Uni Learning. "Academic Writing. The Passive Voice." *uow.edu.au*,

unilearning.uow.edu.au/academic/3avi.html. Accessed 11 August 2017.

University of Toronto. "Passive Voice: When to Use It and When to Avoid It." *utoronto.ca*,

advice.writing.utoronto.ca/revising/passive-voice/. Accessed 10 August 2017.

Yourdictionary. "Active vs. Passive Voice." *yourdictionary.com*,

www.yourdictionary.com/index.php/pdf/articles/192.activevspassivevoice.pdf. Accessed 10

August 2017.

1.4. How to Write in Academic Style

This chapter provides information about peculiarities of the academic style of writing. It was already discussed that it differs from non-academic style by certain features such as the usage of passive voice, and general types of papers it is used in. Now, academic style will be described in more detail. In order to successfully write academic papers, it is important to know how to organize the writing, which sentence structure to choose, and how to create evidence-based research where credible ideas are combined with personal visions of the present author.

A paper written in academic writing style has to include:

- ***An objective manner of narration.***

Instead of first person, a third person narration is used.

> *The research points that…*
>
> *It must be admitted…*
>
> *The paper proves that…*

- ***A correct usage of tenses.***

It is important to keep one tense throughout the whole work. If you write in the present tense, be sure that the whole narration will be in the present. The same applies to the past tense. What is more, pay attention to things that are described. If a discussion is about historical events or something that happened in the past, it is better to write in the past tense. If issues have an impact on the present, the tense can also be present.

> The present tense: *Taylor admits that…*

Taylor's research gives the view of…

<u>The past tense:</u> *The Great Depression had an impact on people's mindsets.*

The study was conducted on five-year-old boys in San Diego.

- ***Appropriate language (depending on the audience).***

Despite the fact that the academic style seems to be more complicated than the non-academic, it does not need to be overloaded with words that are too long or sentence constructions too complex. A specific vocabulary is important, but it should be incorporated in the paper carefully.

All in all, the work has to be readable and understandable for the particular audience. If the paper is addressed to students, use less complicated words or provide explanations. If the paper is for scholars, be precise to show a good understanding of all specific words.

In the Academic Writing Avoid

1. **Contractions.**

   Instead of writing *can't, mustn't, doesn't, won't,* use the full words *can not, must not, does not, will not.*

2. **Short names of words.**

   Instead of saying *TV, phone, quote,* write *television, telephone, quotation.*

3. **Informal words or phrases.**

   Instead of *Taylor's study is fine,* use *Taylor's study is important because…*

   Instead of writing *get through it,* write *survive.*

   Instead of *get, a lot, good, bad,* write *obtain, many, beneficial, incorrect.*

4. **Phrasal verbs.** Examples are *put up with, get away with, get off.*

5. **Run-on expressions.** Examples: *etc., and so on, and so forth.* Compare:

   Informal: *Apart from seeing a psychologist, the right treatment against depression includes a proper diet, physical exercises, taking hobbies, doing meditation, etc.*

   Formal: *Apart from seeing a psychologist, the right treatment against depression includes such activities as a proper diet, physical exercises, taking hobbies, and doing meditation.*

6. **Rhetorical questions.** Compare:

   Informal: *Fast food leads to obesity and diabetes, so why do people still eat it?*

   Formal: *The question concerning an influence of fast food on the appearance of obesity and diabetes still remains.*

7. **Brackets, exclamation marks, or dashes.**

8. **Direct questions.**

9. **Too much personal language.** Examples: *I, we, my.*

10. **Emotive language.**

11. **Incomplete sentences.**

   The talented musician from California. The famous director from Hollywood.

12. **Very long sentences.** These types of sentences should be divided into two.

13. **Wordy sentences.** Compare:

   *A **wordy sentence**: According to the research Sean Taylor made in 2016 while in Mexico, an overpopulation of big cities in poor areas leads to the deterioration of health conditions of the people and a decrease of natural provisions, leaving people stumped as to how to maintain a healthier mode of living for future generations.*

   *A **concise sentence**: Taylor's research conducted in Mexico (2016) showed that when overpopulation happens in poor areas, people face problems that negatively affect health conditions and the abundance of natural provisions.*

14. **Vague words and phrases.**

   If words such as *it*, *they*, and *them* are used, it is important to state previously about what or whom the point is.

   The words *ideas* and *people* are initially vague. It is significant to mention what kind of people and which ideas the author means.

   Do not use phrases such as *in the past* and *in recent days*. The narration should be more specific.

15. **Cliche phrases.** Examples: *time will tell, a matter of time, at the speed of light.*

16. **Too strong of an opinion of material.** This may make your writing look subjective. Compare:

   ***Too strong of an opinion (subjective)**: Taylor's research is so good that it is very important for our discussion.*

   *A **clear, objective opinion**: Taylor's research is valid enough to be significant for our discussion based on the evidence provided.*

   Avoid words like *really, definitely, extremely, quite.*

17. **Taboo language.**

18. **Stereotypes, generalization, assumptions.** This refers to groups different by gender, race, sexuality, and political or religious beliefs.

   Instead of *mankind* write *humankind.*

   Instead of *policeman* use *police officer.*

Other Features to Consider

I. An academic paper should be divided into paragraphs.

II. Paragraphs should be connected by connecting words and phrases such as:

> *in addition to this / what is more / as a result / however / furthermore / then / but / while / in case / provided that.*

III. Put your discussion in a wider circle of studies on a similar subject. In this regard, be as polite towards other opinions as possible.

> Instead of saying *this statement is wrong due to the fact that…* write: *It turns out that… It should be stated that… It appears that…*

IV. Every word should be carefully chosen for its place.

> Instead of *operation against abortion* it is better to say *campaign against abortion.* The word *operation* holds a meaning of some force that is applied to something while the word *campaign* refers to actions that can be used without force or power.

V. Every word should count.

> **Improper usage of words:** *Those who have anorexia should be put into hospitals and receive a relevant medical treatment.*
>
> **Proper usage of words:** *Anorexic patients should be hospitalized for receiving a relevant medical treatment.*

VI. Grammar, the spelling of words, punctuation, and formatting should be perfect. It is important to always keep in mind instructions to every particular assignment since in them a format for the paper is stated (MLA / APA / Chicago). According to the format, the execution of documents is different.

VII. Each academic writing style implies correct referencing. As was stated before, references to credible sources are a must. It is important to support every argument by mentioning other researchers who work with the subject of interest. In this way, a paper enters a broader context and can be used as a part of other scientific projects. Every format has its particular citation rules.

> **MLA**: (citations listed based on author and rules of the format, followed by the name of the resource in parentheses)
>
> > *As it is described, "The pure constituents in these oils stimulate olfactory receptors and activate regions in the brain's limbic system associated with memory, emotion, and state of mind" (Young Living).*

APA: (citations listed based on author and rules of the format, followed by the year of publication if available in parentheses)

> *As experts state, "The production of urine involves highly complex steps of excretion and re-absorption. This process is necessary to maintain a stable balance of body chemicals" (National Kidney Foundation, 2017).*

Chicago (footnotes at the end of every citation and on the bottom of the page)

> *These dimensional characters are enough because of the young age of the patient.[1]*

All in all, academic styles of writing have their peculiarities that have to be considered for successful work performance. They all together make scholarly papers different from other writings and keep them as a separate scientific field stable and comprehensible for all users.

---

[1]

American Academy of Pediatrics, Committee on Quality Improvement and Management and Subcommittee on Attention-Deficit/Hyperactivity Disorder. ADHD: Clinical Practice Guideline for the Diagnosis, Evaluation, and Treatment of Attention-Deficit/ Hyperactivity Disorder in Children and Adolescents. *Pediatrics* 2011:128:000.

Works Cited

Birmingham City University. "Academic Writing Style." *bcu.ac.uk,*

    library.bcu.ac.uk/learner/writingguides/1.20.htm. Accessed 14 August. 2017.

Cambridge Proofreading LLC. "Tips For Writing in an Academic Tone and Style." *proofreading.org,*

    proofreading.org/blog/tips-for-writing-in-an-academic-tone-and-style/. Accessed 14 August.

    2017.

De Montfort University Leicester. "How to Write in an Academic Style." *dmu.ac.uk,*

    www.library.dmu.ac.uk/Support/Heat/index.php?page=488. Accessed 14 August. 2017.

Gillett, Andy. "Features of Academic Writing." *uefap.com,*

    www.uefap.com/writing/feature/intro.htm. Accessed 14 August. 2017.

Chapter 2. Essay Writing Structure

All academic essays should be built on a specific structure. It helps to logically organize a narration and consistently present a discussion concerning a subject of interest. Specifically, the development of academic writing boils down to a combination of relevant ideas into a coherent set of arguments. In this chapter of our guide you will learn about major tasks every essay needs to be written with: introduce an argument, analyze facts, provide counter arguments, and conclude given information.

You will find out that any academic writing consists of specific parts, each of which is designed to carry out the mentioned tasks:

- In the ***introduction*** an argument is introduced.
- In the ***main body*** facts are analyzed and strengthened with counter arguments.
- In the ***conclusion*** given data is summarized.

All academic essays have a fixed introduction and conclusion. Conversely, other parts can change their places. For instance, counterarguments may appear either in each paragraph after an argument of this section is discussed, or they can be separated in one period towards the end of the main body of an essay. Background information (such as historical and biographical context and definitions of terms) should be given at the beginning of an essay, right after the introduction and before the main body.

You will learn how to develop a strong introduction and conclusion, and particular usage of vocabulary can make them better. Also, our examples of common mistakes will point out problematic issues so that you can avoid them in your writing.

In addition to this, this chapter provides ideas of how to fill each part correctly with needed information and how to develop ideas for writing about a subject that seems to be too complicated. You will learn a particular scheme that suits any academic essay, with the help of which you can develop cohesive, logical writing.

2.1. Essay Structure: General Tips

Any essay presents a vast amount of information. In order to organize it and make the narration clear, it is helpful to divide a written work into parts. No matter how big or short an essay is, it should complete several tasks:

- Introduce an argument.

- Analyze facts.

- Provide counter arguments.

- Conclude given information.

Only the introduction and conclusion have stable places in the essay; other sections can be changed. Now let us look closer at the parts of an essay, their functions, and the questions that they answer.

Essay Parts and Questions They Answer

Four previously mentioned aims are completed in three parts:

Introduction (the argument is announced). It normally takes no more than 30 percent of the entire paper.

Body paragraphs (facts are analyzed, and counter arguments are given). It normally takes approximately 40 to 50 percent of the entire paper.

Conclusion (findings are summarized). It normally takes up to 20 to 30 percent of the entire paper.

There are three questions on which an essay has to answer:

"***What?***" This claims from the writer support for the thesis with valid evidence. Basically, an author should support the point of view with credible information and explain why such an opinion was reached. The best place to do so is at the beginning of an essay, right after the thesis statement. It is important to make the answer to this question concise. It should not take more than a third of the essay. If it is bigger than that, a written work will look like a simple description or summary.

"***How?***" This question introduces the counter arguments. It is important to show the reader how a thesis statement deals with opposite views on a subject of interest. When an author gives different opinions, it becomes clear how a thesis varies when it is supported by other ideas. In addition to this, a reader sees other possible thesis statements and views on the issue. A section that answers this question may be given towards the end of an essay. If there are several counter arguments to each argument, it is possible to put them one by one after each argument. This gives the reader an opportunity to think and make a personal opinion towards what was said.

"***Why?***" The writer should show why his or her view is generally important and why it should be considered. This question broadly addresses a thesis statement. It also helps to put research into a more comprehensive context. The significance of an essay is determined by how well this question is answered. It is better to do this at the very end of a written work, in the conclusion, or gradually reply to it throughout the whole paper.

Mapping the Essay

In order to make a good structure for an essay, it is important to analyze a thesis statement and think about things a reader wants to know from it. Surely, he would like to know background information, counter arguments, and an analysis of primary or secondary sources. While mapping out an essay, it is better to focus on sections rather than paragraphs since they give a wider outlook. These are important things for consideration during planning a written work.

A thesis statement should take no more than one or two sentences. Otherwise, it would be too difficult for understanding. After it is stated, it is helpful to support it with a sentence where the importance of such a view is mentioned. In other words, a reader should receive full comprehension of what he will learn from a written work. This section touches upon the question, "Why?" which will be fully answered in conclusion.

After the thesis statement and its supportive explanation are introduced, a further narration can be started with sentences such as:

In order to be convinced by the opinion proposed, the first thing that a reader needs to know boils down to…

The proposed opinion finds its validity through…

The discussion concerning the opinion proposed should be started with…

Concerning the opinion proposed, the reader needs to be shown with…

All these sentences help to introduce supportive arguments. In addition to this, an answer to the question, "What?" begins in this section. According to the purpose of an essay and amount of material that should be proposed, an author can decide that the main body of a written work has to be started with some background information.

It is also useful to keep a verbal connection with the reader by using such narrative sentences:

Another thing the reader needs to know…

It is also important for a reader to consider…

Also, the reader must be informed that…

Keep in mind that every argument has to answer the question, "Why?" and be supported by some evidence.

All in all, the map of an essay should answer three questions and touch upon major ideas that need to be presented. However, it is flexible, so points can move from one section to another (as it was mentioned about counter arguments).

Development of Ideas

In order to write a good, easy-to-read essay that is logically sound, the ideas have to be clear and interact with each other. There are two aspects that have to be considered.

Cohesion. In cohesive writing, ideas flow from one to another. Specifically, they are connected on the sentence level, paragraph level, and full-text level. The writer uses different sentence structures which best serve for narration. Also, the author pays attention to punctuation and makes well-constructed paragraphs. Linking words are helpful in this regard.

Coherence. Coherent writing consists of logically connected ideas that are justified by examples and reasons. In such a way, the reader has an ability to understand all aspects of a subject and see the broader context in which research is placed.

The central idea can always be described in one sentence. It has to answer to the title. Look at the example:

The title: *The Role of Anxiety in Social Relations.*

The central idea: *How does anxiety affect the social life of a person?*

Since the central idea can be described in the form of a question, it should be clearly answered with the help of valid reasoning. For one supportive point, one rationale is needed. Such a cohesive way of narration will naturally lead to a concluding paragraph or counter arguments that can be stated before it.

Paragraph Structure

Since the introduction and conclusion take two separate paragraphs, let us focus on the body of a written work. The amount of paragraphs in it depends on how many arguments there are. Specifically, each paragraph responds to one idea. Imagine that there are four rationales that prove the thesis statement. At that rate, there should be four paragraphs in the body. The structure may seem like the following:

Paragraph 1. Topic sentence A (argument 1).

First justifying sentence.

Second justifying sentence.

Third justifying sentence.

Concluding sentence A.

Paragraph 2. Topic sentence B (argument 2).

First justifying sentence.

Second justifying sentence.

Third justifying sentence.

Concluding sentence B.

Paragraph 3. Topic sentence C (argument 3).

First justifying sentence.

Second justifying sentence.

Third justifying sentence.

Concluding sentence C.

Paragraph 4. Topic sentence D (argument 4).

First justifying sentence.

Second justifying sentence.

Third justifying sentence.

Concluding sentence D.

Paragraph 5. Counter arguments.

Counter argument 1.

Counter argument 2.

Counter argument 3.

Counter argument 4.

It is suggested to have at least three justifying sentences since three rationales provide enough credibility. In the mentioned structure, counter arguments were separated into the last paragraph in the body. Pay attention to the fact that the amount of counter arguments is equal to the number of arguments. As was stated before, it is possible to end every paragraph with them. In this way, they should be put after the third justifying sentence. Every concluding sentence is connected with the topic sentence and thesis statement.

Generally, all mentioned tips help to formulate a well-developed essay structure. In such a way, the student clearly sees his future written work and all parts of it that demand attention. It is recommended to make plans for every essay so that no idea will be missed.

Works Cited

Boundless.com. "Writing." *boundless.com*, www.boundless.com/writing/textbooks/boundless-writing-textbook/writing-effective-paragraphs-253/organizing-your-ideas-258/topic-sentences-127-7913/. Accessed 17 Aug. 2017.

Harvard University. "Essay Structure." *harvard.edu*, writingcenter.fas.harvard.edu/pages/essay-structure. Accessed 17 Aug. 2017.

Monash University. "Logical Development of Ideas." *monash.edu.au*, www.monash.edu.au/lls/llonline/writing/general/academic/3.5.xml. Accessed 17 Aug. 2017.

Newcastle University. "Idea Development." *ncl.ac.uk*, www.ncl.ac.uk/students/wdc/learning/academic/idea.htm. Accessed 17 Aug. 2017.

Uni Learning. "How Is an Essay Structured?" *uow.edu.au*, unilearning.uow.edu.au/essay/4bi.html. Accessed 17 Aug. 2017.

2.2. Essay Introduction Writing

The Role of the Introduction

For many students, creating introductions and conclusions appears to be nearly the most difficult task. It is often easier to determine what things have to be told in the body of the paper than to figure out how to sneak up on them. One recommendation which might be helpful is that it is allowable to write the main part of the essay first. By doing so, the student sees the development of his or her subject and can think about better introductory statements and conclusions.

The introduction gets the reader into a discussion that takes place in the paper. By this introduction section, the audience makes the first impression of the work, its style, and the quality of arguments. It is insufficient just to state arguments because they can be driven from nowhere. They make sense only when the reader sees why they appear and why their presence is important. Therefore, introductions and conclusions are helpful.

With the help of the introduction, the reader receives a chance to take his or her mind off of personal life and concentrate on a scientific subject. Despite the thesis statement that determines the focus of the paper, a good introduction contains some background information that also gives the reader a chance to learn more. For example, if the paper is about the War of Secession (1861-1865), it is important to mention prerequisites such as the expansion of states and the publishing of *Uncle Tom's Cabin*, written by Harriet Beecher Stowe.

When the introduction effectively helps readers to redirect attention from their private lives to a particular research moment, the author can be sure that the audience has been hooked and given tools necessary to delve into the topic.

It is also significant to consider that good introductions may vary depending on the type of paper and academic discipline to which it is related.

The introduction does not have a limited volume, but it should be as brief as possible. It has to end with a thesis statement and a stated research problem. A good introduction shows how a student will address the research issue and in what aspect this approach is unique.

Advice on How to Write an Introduction

Start with questions that should be addressed in the paper. They will be answered throughout the work, but it is helpful to give a clue about them in the introductory section. A direct answer to the questions will be in the thesis statement which concludes the introduction. It is helpful to develop a speculative strategy. It can look like this:

With the knowledge that members of one family have to be naturally supportive towards each other, look how a situation is different in Henry James' Washington Square. Describe in detail what kind of "family damage" the author shows concerning such questions:

What is the family damage itself?

Where does the damage firstly occur?

Why did it appear?

To which consequences does it lead?

Was it possible to prevent it?

How is the damage in the Sloper family relate to social issues of 19th century America?

These questions come from the reading and allow the author to present his personal point of view. What is more, they put the topic about family problems into a bigger context, so a historical background should also be mentioned. Such an argumentative plan allows an author to make the discussion consistent and gradually capture the attention of the readers.

The discussion in a paper should start with broader questions and then come to specific ones. The introduction can also be made by the same principle. The first two sentences may be about general issues, while others touch upon more particular points. To understand the right sequence, it is helpful to look at the instructions for the assignment.

Despite the fact that any discussion should go from general to concrete issues, too broad of information should be avoided. For example, in the mentioned assignment, there is no need to touch upon the biography of Henry James. The context is important, but it should be directly associated with main questions of the discussion. No spare information is needed since it can confuse the reader.

It is recommended to write the introduction in the last turn. The thesis statement may be created right away because it helps not to lose the train of thought. Nevertheless, when all concrete issues are answered throughout the paper in the right way, it is easier to relate them to broader points. Sometimes it is difficult for students to develop all arguments at once. In such a way, the introduction may seem faulty and disturb the overall order of narration.

Since an essay consists of separate parts, they can be written in a changeable order. Every academic paper is a work of research, so by writing it a student studies a particular subject. When he gets a better understanding of arguments and supportive claims, he sees the starting point of the discussion.

As was mentioned before, the introduction makes the first impression of the paper. It has to catch the reader's attention. This can be done with the help of:

- *An intrigue.* Readers will be interested if the author starts the discussion by stating a refutation to some well-known, valid truth claimed by researchers.

- *A provocative question or a famous quote. Family is supposed to be our safe haven. Very often, it is the place where we find the deepest heartache* (Iyanla Vanzant).

- *An anecdote. Oh, I am sorry. I forgot. I only exist when you need something* (a sarcastic anecdote about family relations).

- **A thought-provoking question.** *Since family is responsible for the upbringing of a child, why does it bring him down so easily?*

The first sentence of the introduction should set the tone of the whole paper. It has to contain useful, maybe unexpected, information so that readers will find it intriguing to them.

Common Mistakes

Since many students pay more attention to the argumentative part of an essay, they underestimate the importance of a good introduction. The following mistakes are common.

- *Too vague of an introduction.* This happens when a student does not completely understand the point and decides just to fill the introductory part of the work.

    For example: *Many families suffer from a misunderstanding between members. It is common for kindred people to fight and hate each other. This is an eternal problem and, unfortunately, there is no way to eliminate it.*

To avoid this mistake, it is better to write the introduction after all important arguments are determined.

- ***An introduction that is made from a restated question.***

    For example: *Despite the fact that families should be built on love, Henry James in his* Washington Square *describes an opposite situation. He shows family damage that takes its origins from an old, almost forgotten conflict. It has appeared because members of the family follow different interests. It led to terrible consequences. Unfortunately, it seems that the damage could not be prevented. There were many similar situations in 19th century America.*

Such an introduction simply states answers on all questions that have to be discussed throughout the whole paper, not only in the introductory section. All ideas look untidy and badly organized.

- ***The dictionary introduction.*** This is made when an author mentions a particular subject and gives its definition afterward. If an explanation is unusual and it is evident that it was created exclusively by an author, it can still be allowed.

    Compare two introductions:

    A bad one: *Family damage happens when relations between members become worse.*

    A good one: *An absence of love results in family damage.*

- ***Too broad of an introduction.*** It gives lots of irrelevant, useless information that disturbs the reader from focusing on a particular subject of the discussion.

    For example: *Despite the fact that families should be built on love, Henry James in his novel* Washington Square *describes an opposite situation. He shows a family damage that takes its origins from an old, almost forgotten conflict. This issue is as old as the hills. However, it seems that with the course of time, some things do not change. Specifically, in the 19th century, damaged American families were as common as they are now. People always fight even within the bounds of their own families.*

- ***An introduction that looks like a book report.*** It provides information about the author, the book written by the author, and the main features of the story. This type looks familiar and very simple. Despite its concise format, such an introduction is bad, since it does not prepare the reader for a thesis statement.

    For example: *The famous novel* Washington Square *was written by Henry James. It was originally published in 1890 in Cornhill Magazine. The literary* *work shows problems within one family where members hate each other. The story was told from a third-person point of view.*

Word Choice and Vocabulary

The most important thing about an introduction is that it should be relevant to the chosen topic. Specifically, it should contain words and phrases that are used in discussions concerning the studied academic field. For example, it is obvious that topics "English and Literature" and "Health and Care" should be written with the help of a different vocabulary.

In all cases, words and phrases should be used carefully to show a sufficient understanding of a topic. Since the introduction part contains a thesis statement, it should be incorporated by special words and phrases. Otherwise, it will be lost among other sentences and the reader will not understand the main claim of the paper.

A thesis statement is a short representation of ideas placed in one or two sentences. It also describes an author's position in relation to the subject.

Examples of Good Thesis Statements

1. *Although people are free to choose their life paths according to personal wills and not domestic influences, in some cases age issues can completely change a personality for the worse.*

2. *Despite the fact that both literary works are fully tragical, they not only depict that different circumstances can lead to equally awful consequences, but also give an understanding of how diverse public views on destiny can be.*

3. *In spite of many experiments which were done and are going to be taken soon, at this stage all researchers see nothing but danger in sugar and products that contain it.*

Examples of Good Introductions

1. *To make a case study of psychopathology, a character from the film* A Beautiful Mind *was chosen. His name is John Nash, and he has a real prototype who was a famous mathematician. The film tells the story of the man's life and describes his career successes which were influenced by his mental health issues. The case study will cover causes that led to the problem, analyze symptoms which can help to identify its name, and propose effective treatments for people with the same diagnosis.*

2. *In the modern world, more and more medical institutions choose to incorporate Electronic Health Record systems (EHR) in their practice. Regardless of the fact that such innovations*

are apparently helpful to healthcare professionals, their implementation seems to be a rather difficult work. Apart from its expensiveness, many other problem points have to be analyzed. This paper will address the most evident ones. Once they are resolved, a sustainable start of EHR usage can be guaranteed.

3. *The profession of nurse is one of the oldest. Despite this fact, some people seem to keep a skeptical attitude towards it thinking that nurses highly depend on doctors, have less competence, and serve just as assistants. In such a way, they neglect the whole concept of nursing because apart from caring it also includes masterful managing and diplomatic skills. Although there is the conception that nurses usually choose such a profession because of a call from their hearts, they need to gain a certain level of knowledge to become real specialists in their field.*

All in all, sentences in the introduction are connected not only by their meaning but also with the help of special transitional phrases. They help to establish a speculative tone of work and flowing manner of narration. In such a way, readers easily go from one idea to another and also build an overall picture of the research in their imaginations.

Works Cited

Explorable. "How to Write an Introduction." *explorable.com*, explorable.com/how-to-write-an-introduction. Accessed 21 Aug. 2017.

IELTS Mentor. "Vocabulary for Academic IELTS Writing Task 2 (Part 1)." *ielts-mentor.com*, www.ielts-mentor.com/49-ielts-vocabulary/vocabulary-for-academic-ielts-writing-task-2/530-vocabulary-for-academic-ielts-writing-task-2-part-1. Accessed 21 Aug. 2017.

Purdue Online Writing Lab. "Tips and Examples for Writing Thesis Statements." *purdue.edu*, owl.english.purdue.edu/owl/resource/545/01/. Accessed 21 Aug. 2017.

The University of North Carolina at Chapel Hill. "The Writing Center. Introductions." *unc.edu*, writingcenter.unc.edu/tips-and-tools/introductions/. Accessed 21 Aug. 2017.

2.3. Essay Discussions (Body Section) Writing

After the introduction of an essay comes the body section. This is the big narrative piece where a student can show all acquired knowledge and convince readers with arguments. As was stated before, the writer should capture readers' attention in the introduction by mentioning crucial points of the study in a tightly developed thesis statement. In the discussion section, the audience expects to see a development of these ideas.

The Role of Discussions

The central function of the main body is to disclose arguments in a coherent and consistent narration and connect the introduction with the conclusion. The discussion section answers all questions that were mentioned in the introduction.

It is important to keep one paragraph for one idea. For this reason, the main argument should be rationally divided into clear concepts. If any of these points have additional sub points, they also need to be described in a separate paragraph. As was discussed previously, it is also possible to finish every subsection with a counter argument. In other cases, all objections should be presented in the last paragraph of the main body.

Advice on How to Write Discussions

It is worth remembering that the amount of body paragraphs depends on the complexity of the thesis statement. If it is simple, three subsections can be more than enough. There are several tips that can help to create good discussions.

Make a plan. Before writing body paragraphs, outline them by pointing out every idea and its argument. For example, here is a thesis statement of a paper: *Despite the fact that college education is an expensive and rather complicated thing, it is worth all expenses and efforts.*

Body paragraphs:

1. Idea: *College education leads to better career opportunities.*

   Supportive argument: *In addition to gaining special knowledge, a student has a possibility to widen his or her outlook.*

2. Idea: *College education correlates with self-development.*

   Supportive argument: *In college, a student learns how to schedule his or her life to incorporate studying, resting, hobbies, friends, work, etc.*

3. Idea: *College years are full of adventures and meetings.*

   Supportive argument: *This is also a part of studying because new people and things bring new experiences.*

4. Idea: *If a person enters an intelligent society once, his or her perception of life will change forever.*

   Supportive argument: *People who receive higher education are more active citizens (they vote more, participate in community events more, donate money to special organizations more), so they form a better society.*

The mentioned thesis statement implies a discussion about benefits of college education. Four body paragraphs observe four advantages with an aim to convince readers that despite evident expenses, education at the university level is a helpful and interesting experience. Each paragraph observes the main argument indicated as a thesis statement but from different points of view.

Pay attention that **the first (topic) sentence of each paragraph should state the main point that will be observed further**. After that, one supportive argument should be added. For example:

To begin with, it is quite evident that a college education leads to better career perspectives. What is more, it not only gives needed knowledge but also widens the outlook.

The first sentence gives an idea while the second one provides an argument that supports the point. Such an approach is beneficial to readers as well as to the writer. It helps to focus right away on a statement that needs development through writing. Also, it gives the audience a clue about issues they will study in this paragraph.

Some important points to consider:

- Not only the second sentence but all sentences are related to the first one (the main idea).

- Ideas are not simple statements or facts. They are disputable issues that need to be supported by valid evidence.

- Valid evidence can be presented in forms of:

    - Paraphrases or quotations from credible sources.

    - Findings, facts, or statistical material from relevant studies.

    - Descriptions of a student's experience.

It is worth noting that different types of essays must have the corresponding appropriate types of evidence. For example, it is not appropriate to use personal narratives in works that do not call for them.

After the idea is proposed and the evidence is given, analysis begins. Here, a student should write the interpretation of a problem. It should not be stated in a personal form if it is not previously allowed in the assignment for the paper. A good analysis shows a great understanding of an issue and convinces readers that the stated idea is valid enough to be accepted.

Despite the fact that every paragraph observes one point of a discussion, all subsections should be interrelated. Special words and phrases that help with this task will be discussed later.

The last sentence of each paragraph should show the significance of the proposed idea to the whole argument (from the thesis statement). In addition to this, it also has to imply a further discussion (point to the next issue which will be observed in the next paragraph).

A good subsection allows readers to look at first and last sentences and understand the writer's point of view. For example:

Another significant issue is that the education at university level is closely connected with self-development. Specifically, students have to understand how to schedule their lives in order to balance between studying, resting, and sometimes working. Due to the fact that many college programs are big, they can demand extra skills and knowledge that can be easily gained through self-education by taking additional courses. What is more, it is also common for students to take part-time jobs while studying. Proper self-organization that rationally divides time between all activities brings a feeling of maturity and widens the view too.

Paragraphs should be connected in a logical order. A new subsection should not repeat already described ideas. A narration needs to always progress to new views.

Common Mistakes

Some students do not like to write plans for their papers, or they impatiently want to enter upon the writing itself. By doing so, they quite often make the following common mistakes.

1. Paragraphs are in the wrong order. This is possible when a sub-point goes before an actual point to which it belongs. For example:

> *Another significant issue is that **it is common for students to take part-time jobs** while studying. Due to the fact that many college programs are big, they can demand extra skills and knowledge that can be easily gained through self-education by taking additional courses. Here we need to admit that **the education at university level is closely connected with self-development.** Specifically, students have to understand how to schedule their lives in order to balance between studying, resting, and sometimes working. **Proper self-organization that rationally divides time between all activities brings a feeling of maturity and widens the view too.***

In this example, a sub-idea about part-time jobs and additional courses goes before the main idea about self-organization. All these issues stay in one paragraph due to their simplicity. The same incorrect order can exist between whole subsections if they present bigger arguments.

2. Every new paragraph begins with the repetition of previously mentioned information. For example:

> (the last sentence of a paragraph): *Proper self-organization that rationally divides time between all activities brings a feeling of maturity and widens the view too.*
>
> (the first sentence of a new paragraph): *The rationally built self-organization is significant because it allows incorporating fun things, such as meetings with new people, traveling, and other adventures.*

There is no need to repeat the importance of self-organization because it was already stated before. It is better to correlate meetings and adventures with the main statement concerning benefits of college education.

3. Paragraphs do not have clear points. Sometimes students do not want or can not properly develop their arguments. They try to fill the narrative space with unrelated information. By doing so, they do not make the writing consistent, so they lose points in grades and make papers difficult for reading.

4. A main point of the paragraph is omitted from the first sentence. It happens when a writer forgets that the readers can not read his or her thoughts or know as much about a subject as the writer. That is why an intention of a discussion needs to be stated. Sometimes it is also helpful to remind readers about previously observed issues. However, this does not mean that an evident repetition is correct (we figured out before that it is not). It is allowable to remind readers about the ongoing arguments by incorporating such phrases:

- *As we stated before…*

- *As was discussed previously…*

- *We should remember our previous statement…*

- *It is worth remembering that…*

These phrases lead readers to already mentioned arguments and make a picture about a discussion clear and full.

Word Choice and Vocabulary

In order to make a good discussion section, it is recommended to use special transition words that connect the ideas expressed in sentences and paragraphs. Some useful essay words and phrases are listed below.

Function	Examples
Adding more information to the mentioned facts	in addition, moreover, furthermore, further, again, what is more, either, neither...nor, in the same way, in fact, really, not only...but also, in reality, it is found that, with respect to, besides, as to, regarding, as for, above all, as well as, due to the fact that
Listing	first(ly), second(ly), third(ly), to begin with, in the second place, another, in addition, additionally, also, then, next, finally, lastly, in conclusion, to conclude
The same ideas described differently	in other words, for instance, for example, that is to say, namely, and, as follows, an example of this is, such as, including, especially, particularly, in particular, mostly, notably, chiefly
Introducing an alternative opinion	nevertheless, however, in spite of, despite, while, after all, although, though, on the other hand, at the same time, all the same, even if

Introducing the results	as a result, the result is, it is evident that, therefore, so, then, it can be seen that, the consequent is that, we can see, because of this, this suggests, it follows that, in other words, for this reason, due to
Concluding stated information	as a conclusion, to conclude, in brief, all in all, therefore, so
Phrases for introducing quotations	<ul><li>According to (*the name of the researcher*), ...</li><li>(*the name of the researcher*) says / shows / admits / suggests that ...</li><li>To quote from (*the name of the researcher*) ...</li><li>Referring to (*the name of the researcher*), he / she argues that ...</li></ul>
Transition phrases within one paragraph	<ul><li>Due to the fact that (*state a previous idea*), this section shows that (*bring a new idea*).</li><li>In order to get a better understanding of (*state a previous idea / a topic of an overall discussion*), this section observes that ... (*bring a new idea*).</li></ul>

All discussed peculiarities regarding the body section of an essay are important for consideration. With the help of described tips, students will be able to understand the purpose of narrative discussions and write better essays.

Works Cited

PennState Abington. "Traditional Academic Essays in Three Parts." *psu.edu*,
abington.psu.edu/traditional-academic-essays-three-parts. Accessed 24 Aug. 2017.

Totten Intermediate School. "Useful Argumentative Essay Words and Phrases." *is34.org*,
www.is34.org/pdfs/Examples_of_Argumentative_Language.PDF. Accessed 24 Aug. 2017.

Uni Learning. "The Body of the Essay." *uow.edu.au*, unilearning.uow.edu.au/essay/4biii.html.
Accessed 24 Aug. 2017.

University of Leeds. "Essay Writing: The Main Body." *leeds.ac.uk*,
library.leeds.ac.uk/info/485/academic_skills/333/essay_writing/5. Accessed 24 Aug. 2017.

Write. Content Solutions. "Avoiding Common Mistakes in Essay Structure." *write.com,*
write.com/writing-guides/assignment-writing/writing-process/avoiding-common-mistakes-in-essay-structure/. Accessed 24 Aug. 2017.

2.4. Essay Conclusions Writing

The Role of Conclusions

In order to finish an essay in the right way, a good conclusion is needed. It gives the writer a final chance to convince readers in his point of view and amaze them with the validity of his arguments. The impression that readers have from the conclusion will stay with them and determine whether the writer is good or bad.

In such a way, the final part of an essay should give a sense of completeness and, at the same time, the feeling that a discussed topic can be prolonged. In one word, a conclusion has to finish a taken discussion but not the whole subject.

The main goal of a conclusion is to sum up everything that was said before. No new ideas are needed.

Advice on How to Write Conclusions

A good conclusion has to meet certain requirements. It should:

1. Reapprove an idea that was mentioned in the thesis statement.
2. Summarize all points of the essay (from the main body).
3. Give the reader an interesting last impression.
4. Confirm the importance of the chosen arguments. This can be done by reaffirmation of the most significant evidence that supports the argument.

In order to write a good conclusion, use one of the following tips:

- Finish an essay by linking the last paragraph to the first. For example, it is possible to use synonyms of words which were used at the beginning of the work.

> **In the introduction:** *People always create dreams. Nevertheless, they do not always believe that wishes can come true. When they suddenly do, a reaction may be unpredictable.*

> **In the conclusion:** *Summarizing the above, it is significant to say that the main idea which the author states comes down to the fact that when a person has a desire for something, even if it is placed in a subconscious part of his mind, he should always be ready to receive what he wants.*

- Use one-syllable (simple) words throughout the whole conclusion. Simple language after a complicated discussion makes things clear.

> *In conclusion, it should be said that sugar consumption is a tricky issue nowadays. Manufacturers use it in large quantities for making a profit from their goods. In such a way, every person has to be responsible for products that enter his or her mouth. There is no need to rely on food corporations. Let us begin with reading labels on goods. This can be the first great step towards the better health of humanity.*

- Create compound sentences. Their balanced structure also looks simpler after a complicated argumentation.

> *With this in mind, anorexia nervosa appears to be a self-inflicted, severe starvation disorder and it affects people drastically nowadays. It is very good that recently people have begun to talk about it freely and have lost their fear or shame of being diagnosed with anorexia. Due to this beneficial fact, doctors can propose better assistance and patients can be healed in a timely manner.*

- Finish with a quotation from a valid resource that was used in the preparation for writing. If necessary, it can reveal a different aspect of a subject. For example, a suitable quotation from a novel which is observed in a paper can give an additional meaning and specify the entire research. Some words of a relevant scholar help to confirm the stated point.

> *Experts admit that the right attitude to food is just one part of the healing process. It is also significant to create a healthy body image. This can be done with the assistance of other people (Garner et al).*

- Set a discussion in a broader context. For example, an essay about *Great Expectations* written by Charles Dickens can be combined with a historical background of the second half of the nineteenth century.

- Finish by addressing one key idea of an argument. For example, an essay about the controversial nature of Caligula can be finished with a comparison of him with other Roman emperors and a calling to read different historical facts, the knowledge of which helps to make an attitude to Caligula as objective as possible.

A good conclusion is built on such a structure:

1. The first sentence restates the thesis statement.

2. The second and third sentences generalize the central ideas of the essay (they were discussed in the main body.

3. The last sentences leave readers with an interesting impression.

A thesis statement: *Expressive arts therapy is not only an interesting task that develops the visual abilities of a child, but also can be used as a healing method for those kids who have psychological problems.*

A conclusion: *In such a manner, it was proven that expressive arts therapy helped to improve mental states of kids during the experiment. In addition to this, the study shows that there is a correlation between a person's psychological condition and physical processes that happen in the body. Specifically, when children were preoccupied with a calm practice of art therapy, cortisol levels in their brains decreased. In such a way, artistic activities are helpful in transforming negative energy into a material object. This sets a mind free and positively affects the whole well-being due to changes in the chemical processes of the body. The taken experiment serves as an additional confirmation that all things in the human organism are connected. That is why it is necessary to study psychology with its correlation to biochemistry.*

As it is evident, the conclusion has no new information. Conversely, it combines all discussed issues and gives readers the ability to think about them. Despite the fact that the content of a conclusion is similar to the content of an introduction, they are not the same. In such a way, it is important to remember that even though the final part restates information from the first part, it does it differently since towards the end of an essay readers know more about the subject than they knew when reading the introduction.

When we talked about the introduction, we stated that this part separates readers from their personal lives and places them in front of the subject of a discussion. Similarly, it is great when a concluding part brings them back in their habitual environment by pointing out how learned information correlates with the actual world around them.

To sum it up so far, the analysis of Willa Cather's "Paul's Case" shows that it is highly significant for a person to be aware of the reality he chooses to live in. Only when it is done, it is possible to focus on things that can be brought to this reality. Unfortunately, it is very difficult to be that conscious in the present world. It is because the lives of people are highly affected by media sources, so it is difficult to choose worthy things from this diversity. At the same time, great art is still present around people. It is always better to be interested in this than in the ever-changing fashions. People should learn how to incorporate artistic works that speak to their souls into their daily routines in a way that eternal beauty gives them the energy to make their usual duties.

Common Mistakes

When students are not patient enough to write a good conclusion, such mistakes can occur:

1. The conclusion is just a summary of discussed arguments. This makes readers confused because such a concluding part repeats the main body of the essay and does not clarify major learning points that were proven.

2. The conclusion gives new information. If the student comes to a conclusion but finds out that there are more arguments to give, it is always better to return to the main body and add them there.

3. The conclusion is only one sentence. The final part has to take approximately 20-30% of the whole essay. It is obvious that in one sentence it is not possible to meet all requirements of a good conclusion.

Word Choice and Vocabulary

Due to the fact that the conclusion presents results and findings made in the essay, such words will be useful:

Function	Examples
points to effect / result / consequence	as a result, for, consequently, under the circumstances, thus, therefore, in that case, for this reason, because of the, then, in effect, hence, thereupon, accordingly, henceforth, forthwith
points to restatement / conclusion / summary	after all, by and large, to sum up, in fact, on the whole, in summary, in conclusion, in any event, in either case, all in all, in short, in brief, in essence, overall, usually, ordinarily,

	to summarize, on balance, altogether, as can be seen, generally speaking, in the final analysis, all things considered, as shown above, in the long run, given these points, as has been noted, in a word, for the most part

This chapter has given the most important peculiarities concerning writing good conclusions. Our tips will help to understand the importance and functions of the final essay section. By taking them into consideration, students learn how to improve their writing and follow it through to the end.

Works Cited

English Language Smart Words. "Transition Words." *smart-words.org*, smart-words.org/linking-words/transition-words.html. Accessed 28 Aug. 2017.

Harvard University. "Ending the Essay: Conclusions." *harvard.edu*, writingcenter.fas.harvard.edu/pages/ending-essay-conclusions. Accessed 28 Aug. 2017.

Math-Hawaii-edu. "How to Avoid Common Mistakes Writing a Term Paper Conclusion." *math-hawaii-edu.net*, math-hawaii-edu.net/avoiding-common-mistakes-when-writing-a-paper-conclusion.html. Accessed 28 Aug. 2017.

Newcastle University. "Writing the Conclusion." *ncl.ac.uk*, ncl.ac.uk/students/wdc/learning/essays/writingessays/conclusion.htm. Accessed 28 Aug. 2017.

Purdue OWL Engagement. "Conclusions." *purdue.edu*, owl.english.purdue.edu/engagement/2/2/60/. Accessed 28 Aug. 2017.

Uni Learning. "The Conclusion of the Essay." *uow.edu.au*, unilearning.uow.edu.au/essay/4biv.html. Accessed 28 Aug. 2017.

The University of North Carolina at Chapel Hill. "The Writing Center. Introductions." *unc.edu*, http://writingcenter.unc.edu/tips-and-tools/introductions/. Accessed 28 Aug. 2017.

Chapter 3. Academic Phrasebook

Due to the fact that academic writing is used for presenting scholarly issues, it works with a specific, defined vocabulary. There are also words from everyday language that are forbidden from appliance in research papers. On top of that, there are words that are peculiar to every scientific field, but some of them are relevant to all academic writings. Such language units are conventional for a scholarly society as a whole. An essay which contains these vocabulary items can be estimated as academic.

Our academic phrasebook is a general source of specific language units for all academic writers. It presents examples of relevant vocabulary according to each section of the essay. This helps writers to easily find a necessary word if they need to fill a narration gap in their writing or connect ideas.

Our academic phrasebook is a collection of sentence frames that contain keywords which are used in specific parts of an essay. What is more, the whole collection is divided into sections in conformity with purposes that should be performed. For instance, the focus is on:

- *Topic sentences* (which forms are better and why).

- *Signposting* (how to use signpost words effectively).

- *Academic words that can be applied in titles* (which academic words used in titles set a frame for a successful scholarly paper).

- *Verbs that are good for academic writing* (which verbs are used for reporting information and citation, how to distinguish verbs with multiple meanings, and which verbs should not be used in academic writing).

- *Phrases* (which phrases are applied for stating an aim, which word units are useful for referencing, and which phrases help to organize data analysis logically).

- *Commonly confused words and ways of implementing them correctly.*

In addition to this, in our phrasebook you will find specific words for arguing, making a claim, presenting data, making a debate, or giving evidence.

Refer to our complete guide to learn all about academic vocabulary that makes your writing better.

3.1. Topic Sentences and Signposting

Topic Sentences

Topic sentences are placed at the beginning of paragraphs. They help readers to understand the core question of a paragraph. By reading them first, the audience guesses which arguments will be proposed. In such a way, topic sentences show a correlation between a thesis statement and its representation in a particular section of an essay. Their usage allows an author to highlight the main points of the writing. Specifically, they argue a statement which then is reported in more detail throughout the whole paragraph.

Topic sentences help to observe a thesis statement from different angles and check whether it is valid or not. That is why it is a good idea to create them right after the main argument was developed.

Forms of Topic Sentences

It should be mentioned that there can be up to three topic sentences in a paragraph. The first sentence **makes a claim**, the second **reflects it**, and the third one **explains it in more detail**.

For example: *Hoffman observes a study that was done by the Professor of Psychology David S. Yeager, at the University of Texas at Austin. He wanted to find out how it is possible to decrease the stress level of new students who just pass in to high school. The scholar figured out that supportive talks and affirmations are not as beneficial as they are thought to be.*

In order to make this three-sentence structure correct, answer such questions before writing:

1. What is your idea?

2. How did your idea appear?

3. Why did this particular idea appear?

Apart from the mentioned scheme, there is no singular method of writing topic sentences. It is recommended that they should vary at least a little bit. In such a way, the essay will not look boring and readers will be interested to proceed, reading each new paragraph as it appears.

There are several types of topic sentences.

- *Complex sentences.* These are sentences that incorporate a transition from the previous paragraph. They usually contain subordinate and independent clauses. Also, they show a transition from old information to new facts.

> **For example:** *Although the anticipation that Beckett depicts in* Waiting for Godot *may prompt a feeling of forthcoming better times, it often seems to be aimless; the focus is lost, and the present is neglected with little hope for the future which may not even come.*

The subordinate clause here (which begins with "although" and ends with "times") correlates with the previous paragraph. The independent clause (which begins with "it" and "the focus") proposes new information — a claim about how the anticipation appears to be ("it often seems to be aimless") and why it appears to be so ("the focus is lost, and the present is neglected with little hope for the future which may not even come").

- *Questions.* Sometimes questions make good topic sentences too. They bring out the idea of a paragraph right away and intrigue readers with the desire to think about it. Due to the fact that they set for a conversation, the author begins the dialog with the audience. While reading an argumentation, readers may also develop their personal views so the reading will be very productive.

> **For example:** *Is it fair to believe that a person is hopeless until he or she understands his or her helplessness?*

Questions are inquiries so they obviously demand answers. In such a way, they are effective especially when a writer wants to highlight personal understanding of a subject into a discussion.

- *Bridge sentences.* This term was founded by John Trimble. They are useful when it is necessary to make a topic sentence more formal. Their name comes from the fact that they serve as a bridge between information that was said before and facts that are going to follow it. No multiple clauses are needed. Bridge sentences are short, brief, and concrete. However, they sometimes repeat what was said before in order to add more information about it.

For example: *But there is an objection to this finding.*

- *Pivots.* This is for a situation when topic sentences do not appear at the beginning of a paragraph but go in the middle of it. It happens when a discussion changes its direction drastically. For example, we mentioned before situations when it is possible to incorporate a counter argument right after the main argument. This is when pivots are useful.

For example: *Specifically, men are close, but Vladimir states that he feels lonely. In such a way, there is a miscommunication between characters and they stay together not for being with each other but for seeing Godot. In order to kill their time, men decide to hang onto one another. Consequently, it is obvious that the situation becomes absurd. **However,** Beckett refers to this way of narration with an aim to show how people spend their time when nothing, in particular, happens around them. **Yet** men perceive time and space differently. They both are bored but they have diverse causes for this boredom. The idea that life is actually meaningless is not new. **But** it is worth remembering that every person implies his personal meaning so it is up to the person what to make out of his or her existence.*

Signposting

Signposts prepare readers for the changes in the direction of arguments. They indicate how far the argumentation goes relating to the thesis statement and claims. Signposts can be used in the form of:

- **A counter argument.** *By contrast, a wrecked brain is likely to support beliefs of others when a refreshed mind has more energy to generate personal thoughts.*
- **A pausing.** This is always used to give scientific or historical background.
  Specifically, scientists were always interested in the sleeping process and its influence on health condition.

Signposts serve as topic sentences for an entire section of an essay. It is because they state ideas that need more than one sentence to be fully described. In longer works, they may take several sections, or in other words, a few paragraphs. They remind readers about the subject of the writing and the purpose of its discussion.

What are signposting sentences? Signposting sentences can be written as one or two sentences at the beginning of a paragraph or be used to connect whole sections of an essay. In the last case, they bridge two parts of an argument together. In such a way, they show how two ideas are related, whether they are similar or contrasting, and whether one idea gives more points about the previous one or concludes it. By meeting signposts, readers follow the author's way of thinking.

For example: *Another supporting point for the immortality of the soul comes down to the fact that it has specific knowledge that turns out to appear much before its latest appearance in the world.* **Less briefly**, *Plato mentions an equality that can be found everywhere.* **Nevertheless**, *a human being understands it only since he knows what it means.*

In this example, the signpost is the first sentence. It begins with the word "another" which introduces one more idea concerning the subject of the discussion. Hence, it not only gives additional information but also reminds readers of the main topic. The next sentence proceeds to talk about this idea while the third one turns out to be the topic sentence of the paragraph. The next subsection starts with the description of Plato's statement that each soul has its memory and so a person acts according to it. In such a way, the signposting sentence is revealed in more detail and the whole section is devoted to one topic so readers can get better knowledge of this particular question without being lost in other arguments concerning immortality.

Signposting sentences can be introduced by specific words. See the list below:

Purpose of Usage	Words	Examples in a Sentence
Introducing a sequence of ideas in an argument	Firstly, Secondly, Thirdly, etc. To begin with Initially Next Then Lastly Finally Subsequently	• **Firstly**, it is important to develop a group of participants… • **Then** methods of a valuation can be established. • **Finally**, the results showed that…
Making a cross-reference to other parts of an essay	As was discussed before As noted above / below As stated previously	• **As was discussed before**, more precise trials are needed. • **As noted above**, the latest of Taylor's findings appeared to be an objection to previously noted theories. • **As stated previously**, the very

			first intention to build this ship came from an American artist named Sean Alan Taylor in 1876.
Giving more ideas / details	Moreover In addition Additionally Also What is more Again Furthermore Besides Indeed Similarly Equally Apart from this		• **In addition to this**, there were no enthusiasts who wanted to share Taylor's dream. • **Similarly**, authorities of the state of California did not support the plan.
Giving an example	For example For instance To illustrate To demonstrate		• **For example**, Taylor did not know shipbuilding very well, so he could not design all of the details of a future ship.
Focusing on a specific detail	Specifically In particular		• **Specifically**, there was no powerful machine that could make that coupling.
Generalizing	In general Generally Usually On the whole In most cases For the most part		• **In general**, the plan was invalid because of many small errors and oversights. • The result is, **in most cases**, controversial.
Introducing a	Similarly		• **Compared with** the first

comparison / the next point for supporting an argument	By the same token In comparison with Compared with In the same way Whereas In like manner Likewise	plan, the next one was definitely better. • **Whereas** the first plan was rather vague, the next one gave more details and calculations.
Introducing the contrast / alternative point	Nevertheless In contrast By contrast Conversely But However Nevertheless Although On the other hand Alternatively On the contrary Yet	• **However**, the result was checked by other scientists too. • **On the other hand**, poetry is more melodic than simple prose. • **Nevertheless**, this seemed to be the best chance so far.
Introducing the fact / stating the obvious	Evidently It is evident that Obviously Clearly Naturally Of course After all	• **Obviously**, a person can not fly. • **It is evident that** some time is needed for symptoms to show themselves. • **Clearly**, the vaccine is very expensive since the disease is rare.
Rephrasing / explaining	In other words Or rather To be more precise To put it in other way / more simply	• **In other words,** a storage unit will be the best place for keeping all things that are used rarely. • **To be more precise,** fill the

	That is to say Namely	form in your personal cabinet online and send us your personal data.
Introducing a reason / result / logical conclusion / proof	Consequently As a consequence Accordingly Due to Thus It could be concluded that Hence For this reason Indeed As a result Therefore Because In fact	• **Consequently,** the police could not enter the house. • **Due to** the hurricane in Texas, many people lost their property. • **For this reason**, it is better to be ready for everything. • **In fact**, it is impossible to control such severe weather conditions.
Concluding	In conclusion To conclude In short To sum up As this essay has demonstrated Finally	• **In conclusion,** it should be said that sometimes people seem to be powerless in front of nature. • **As this essay has demonstrated**, sometimes several decades have to pass before a great idea finds its implementation.

Signposting sentences can be used at the beginning of a paragraph, in its middle, or at the end. They can indicate the function of a section according to the main argument that was stated. It is important to use signposting words carefully since they easily change the meaning of writing.

Compare these two sentences:

- *He always dreamed of being a writer. **However**, he did not enter the university.*

- *He always dreamed of being a writer.* **For this reason**, *he did not enter the university.*

Topic sentences and signpost words serve as important parts of essay structure. With the help of them, an author can make significant accents, lead readers deeply in the topic, and connect all sections of an essay in a concise and logical way.

Works Cited

Exploring U.S. History. *"Bridge Sentences." ou.edu,* explorehistory.ou.edu/wp-content/uploads/2013/08/Bridge-Sentences.pdf. Accessed 30 Aug. 2017.

Harvard University. "Topic Sentences and Signposting." *harvard.edu,* writingcenter.fas.harvard.edu/pages/topic-sentences-and-signposting. Accessed 30 Aug. 2017.

University of East Anglia. "Using 'Signpost' Words and Phrases." *uea.ac.uk,* portal.uea.ac.uk/documents/6207125/7632456/using+signpost+words+and+phrases.pdf/4347566d-8b81-49ed-b715-e98d28467fed. Accessed 30 Aug. 2017.

3.2. Writing Essay Titles

We have already discussed how to write certain parts of an academic essay and what words, phrases, and sentence structures to use. However, any essay begins with a title. It goes even before an introduction, so it is responsible for the very first impression the reader creates about the work. The title will tell the audience whether the essay is worth reading or not. It can capture the reader's attention or leave them untouched. In such a way, it is important to create a valid and intriguing heading which can serve as a great framing for work. This section of our guidebook will be helpful for those students who struggle with choosing a suitable topic for their essays.

Mistakes to Avoid

- **The absence of a title.** When an essay remains without a name, readers do not receive the possibility of understanding the purpose of the work. They are unable to become interested. If they proceed reading, the chance that they will make it to the conclusion is still low. Without a name, an essay is not finished. Never underestimate the power of a title.

- **Making an assignment sequence as a title.** Something like *Essay #1* is a big mistake. Even if the present work correlates somehow with the previous one, it is necessary to state in what ways they are related.

   Essay #1: The Sweeter Your Food, the More Bitter Your Life: How Sugar Provokes Heart Diseases

Essay #2: The Sweeter Your Food, the More Bitter Your Life: How Sugar Leads to Obesity

- **Naming an essay according to its type.** Something like *Narrative Essay* or *Descriptive Essay* can not be estimated as a sufficient title.

- **Giving too generalized a name.** For example, the title *Analysis of Lord Byron's Poetry* seems too boring, too simple, and too broadly-based. More than likely, the essay focuses on particular poems that are linked by a certain motif or theme. It is a good idea to point to this in the title.

Oriental Motifs in Lord Byron's Poetry

Theme of Loneliness in Lord Byron's Poetry

Slavic Sentiments in Lord Byron's Poem "Mazeppa"

In such a manner, titles have to be specific so readers can guess the main subject of the essay from the first sight.

How to Develop Title Ideas

A good title refers to the context of the essay. It not only states the subject but also provides some additional ideas. These ideas concern the following:

- **The tone of the essay** (whether it is formal or more casual).

- **The structure of the essay** (whether something was compared or described, or contrasted in the paper).

- **The writer's opinion** (whether the author supports the subject or argues against it).

Before we discuss how to develop good names for essays, it is important to state criteria which they have to meet. So a presentable heading:

- **Points to a subject.** Too general, boring, and obvious headings do not identify the subject. On the contrary, titles that are specific enough and reflect a topic of writing give enough information about the work itself. Compare:

Vague Headings	Specific and Intriguing Headings
Oedipus	*The Downfall of Oedipus as God's Punishment*
Othello	*The Self-Inflicted Catastrophe of Othello*
The Effect of Sleeping on a Person's Memory	*The Influence of Sleep Restriction and Sleep Deprivation in Producing False Memories*

- Indicates the tone of the paper. Headings show readers the level of seriousness of the essay. For example, direct titles such as *The Policy Recommendation* and *Nursing Philosophy* state that essays should be perceived seriously. At the same time, a heading like *Tips for the Best Vacation in Huntington Beach, CA* points out that the information presented in the paper is not only educative but also entertaining.

- Specifies a particular issue of the subject. For more information look above (examples of headings concerning Lord Byron's poetry, the first section of this chapter).

- Refers to a particular reader. Good titles have to be interesting and intriguing to people who are familiar with the subject. Valid headings should indicate to whom an essay is written. Obviously, serious titles should frame papers on significant problems. Moreover, readers from a specific scientific field have probably read works on your subject before. Your essay should be attractive enough so they want to read it. A good heading helps to capture their attention.

Tips for Creating a Good Title

1. Use a sentence (its transformation) from an essay that reflects its main idea.

The subject of the essay: modern education.

The main idea: With technological devices people have become different: they demand more, get distracted easily, and welcome changes quickly. Professors should transform their methods of education in order to keep students interested.

The title: One the Way Forward: Ways to Educate the Youth in the Changing Digital World

2. Write a heading that begins with words *When*, *How*, *What*, *Who*, *Where*, or *Why*. Such titles always look intriguing and interesting.

How to Deal With Anxiety

When the Sun Goes Down

What Will Be in the World in 400 Years: Predictions of Contemporary Philosophers and Theologians

Who Is in Charge for Capital Punishment

Where Electronic Health Records Have to Be Implemented

Why People Stop Eating: Anorexia Nervosa as a Mental Disorder

3. Write a title that begins with *Do*, *Does*, *Will*, *Is*, or *Are*. Such words make questions. Headings that pose questions explicitly address readers and energize them into a dialog.

Do People Enjoy Talks about Politics?

Does Trump Support Connections with Russia?

Will the Environmental Issues Be Solved by the Early 22nd Century?

Is the Abortion One Solution Against Teen Pregnancy?

Are Schizophrenic People Afraid of Their Phantoms?

4. Use a concrete image from the essay. Use something that readers can imagine themselves.

The Fresh Air of a Winter Night

The Hot Sun of California

5. Use an unusual image from an essay.

A Killing Joy

An Undreamt Baby

6. Make a title provocative.

Why Franz Kafka Avoided Eating Meat

Why I Do Not Believe in God

7. Make a famous quotation your heading. If you do so, always refer to whom the saying belongs.

8. Sum up the main points of the essay in several words.

Context, Form, and Content

Feminism, Freedom, and Single-Sex Education

As we see, there are plenty of ideas that are helpful in the creation of an unusual, catching title. Use any of them according to subject, tone, and type of essay.

Academic Words to Use

Sometimes titles are more complicated and contain specific academic vocabulary. If there is a need of making deep research concerning a subject of interest, it is recommended to use the words listed below:

Academic Words	Explanations / Purpose of Usage	Examples
Accounting for	Explaining why something happens.	*Accounting for the Latest Hurricane in Texas*
Comparing	Showing the similarity between two or more issues.	*Comparing* Oedipus *and* Othello
Contrasting	Showing differences between two or more issues.	*Contrasting Capitalism and Communism*

Arguing	Stating arguments for and against a subject of interest and expressing a writer's point of view.	*Arguing for Birth Control Methods*
Critically evaluating	Analyzing arguments for and against a subject of interest and stating their strong and weak points.	*Critical Evaluation of Religious Sects and Church*
Evaluating	Observing the validity of a subject of interest with supportive evidence.	*Evaluating Veganism as an Environmentally Healthy Way of Eating*
Defining	Presenting the concrete meaning of a subject of interest.	*Defining Film Noir*
Examining	Studying a subject of interest in detail.	*Examination of American Classic Movies in the 1930s*
Describing	Giving detailed information concerning a subject of interest.	*Describing Modern British Poetry Since the Beginning of the 2000s*
Identifying	Briefly explaining some details of a subject of interest.	*Identifying Pros and Cons of Essential Oils*
Distinguishing	Identifying diverse sides of several objects.	*Distinguishing the Best Sugar Substitute Products*
Explaining	Giving valid information of why a subject of interest happens or why it is that particular way.	*Explaining the Influence of Depression on Physical Health*
Discussing	Writing the most important characteristics of a subject of	*Discussing Obsessive Compulsive Disorder*

	interest.	
Illustrating	Giving visual or verbal explanations of a subject of interest.	*Illustrating Ways of Coping with Procrastination*
Justifying	Proving with evidence.	*Justifying Physical Exercises as a Helpful Treatment Against Depression*
Interpreting	Explaining the importance of a subject of interest and evidence that correlates with it.	*Interpreting the Effect of Classical Music on the Human Brain*
Outlining	Giving the main points only.	*Outlining American History of the 19th Century*
Stating	Giving the main features simply and briefly.	*Stating Benefits of Fruit Consumption*
Reviewing	Analyzing a subject of interest from its key points.	*Reviewing Sean Taylor's Research*
Tracing	Looking at the process of development of a subject of interest.	*Tracing the History of Television*
Summarizing	Giving main points and omitting details.	*Summarizing Sean Taylor's Latest Study*
Analyzing	Examining a subject of interest in very deep details.	*Analyzing Study Results From UCLA*

All these words help to make titles clear to readers. Specifically, they indicate the main purpose of an essay and show whether it will discuss, describe, argue, or outline information. However, headlines with such defining elements seem very plain. They do not intrigue but only point to the main purpose of the work. If an essay allows making a title more interesting, it is better to use this possibility.

All in all, the title plays a significant role in the success of an essay. Use our tips for creating a worthy name for your work. Be precise, creative, and moderate in equal measure.

Works Cited

De Montfort University Leicester. "Glossary of Academic Words Used in Titles." *dmu.ac.uk*, library.dmu.ac.uk/Support/Heat/index.php?page=467. Accessed 6 Sept. 2017.

Kibin. "How to Write Good Essay Titles That Are… Good." *kibin.com*, kibin.com/essay-writing-blog/how-to-write-good-essay-titles/. Accessed 6 Sept. 2017.

University of Minnesota. "Writing an Effective Title." *writing.umn.edu*, writing.umn.edu/sws/assets/pdf/quicktips/titles.pdf. Accessed 6 Sept. 2017.

3.3. Verbs for Academic Writing

As was discussed before, the main purpose of an academic essay is to present a new outlook on a certain problem. Academic writing contains many substantives that indicate particular things. Thuswise, they obviously need strong verbs to be accompanied with. Verbs help to organize facts that have to be presented and move a narration from one argument to another. Of course, it is possible to refer to common verbs in academic writing (such as *have, be, find, get*), but the usage of more specific words is a better show of knowledge for a student.

It is helpful to remember that every widely-used verb has its more rare synonym. In order to find out whether it is appropriate to your subject or not, check it with a dictionary.

As we remember from previous chapters of our guide, in academic writing verbs can be used in active or passive voices. What is more, their grammatical forms depend on the purpose of the section where they are applied.

Verb Tenses According to Writing Purpose

In academic writing, it is advisable to use simple present, simple past, and present perfect verb tenses. Sometimes it is also possible to use present continuous and present perfect continuous. The usage of a particular tense depends on the time of the action that has to be described. The right appliance of verb forms describes the correct sequence of events which provides smooth and logical narration.

If an exposition of arguments began in the past tense, it is better to hold to this tense throughout the entire writing. In the same way, if the present tense was chosen from the very beginning, keep it accordingly.

Different sections of an essay demand diverse verb appliances. Specifically, verbs are used for:

- **Explanation** (why and how the subject of interest happens).
- **Narration** (reports a sequence of events, arguments, or results concerning the subject of interest).
- **Description** (gives more details concerning the subject of interest).
- **Argumentation** (convinces readers to accept a writer's point of view).

Explanations can be given in past, present, or future tenses.

*1. The purpose of this study **was** to observe how different styles of music affect memory capabilities of first-year students.*

*2. The aim of the paper **is** to find out a correlation between the amount of work and anxiety that office employees have.*

*3. The main goal of the research **will be** to analyze the influence of historical events on the artwork of Victor Marie Hugo.*

Narration can be presented with the help of present or past tenses. It is always in the form of reported speech. When we talk about researchers of the past and their works, we can also use the present tense. In this way, we refer to a historical present.

- *Taylor (2016) **reported** that previously made results **were** rather contradictory.*
- *Taylor (2016) **reports** that previously made results **are** rather contradictory.*
- *Taylor (2016) **reports** that previously made results **were** rather contradictory.*

Description, in most cases, is written in the present tense (present simple, continuous, and perfect tenses).

- *Investments in this field **have** a daily kind.*
- *New amendments to the local law **have evoked** a mass resistivity.*
- *In order to make the concert in December, the whole band **is practicing** for four or six hours every day now.*

Argumentation presents the position of the writer and states pros and cons of the arguments. It usually combines different tenses. For example:

*Concerning a possible cure, experts **suggested** the appliance of antipsychotic medications. They control the dopamine level and **are** effective even in small doses. Antidepressants and anti-anxiety drugs **may be** helpful too. If a patient has an intolerance towards pills,* *they **can be** replaced by injections. Fortunately, it **has been found** that modern generations of medication **cause** less discomfort and serve almost all patients. In addition to this, researchers have understood that family therapy or social training is necessary too.*

Common Verbs in Academic Writing

As a particular field of writing, academic narration gives itself away by common words that are conventional and go from one work to another. The table below presents certain verbs that are acceptable in academic essays concerning all disciplines. It is important to note that mentioned verbs are not just synonyms. They have different shades of meaning that vary according to the context.

Purpose of Verbs	Examples
A demonstration of stability	sustain, maintain, contain, support
A demonstration of a change or difference	<ul><li>Decreasing: deteriorate, reduce, decline, minimize, narrow, worsen, erode</li><li>Increasing: optimize, exceed, improve, maximize, broaden, generate, enlarge</li><li>Varying: contrast, deviate, alter, convert, evolve, differentiate, transform, differ, diverge, revise, distinguish, modify</li></ul>
A demonstration of limits	restrict, inhibit, prohibit, confine
A demonstration of detailed trial	examine, observe, survey, investigate, analyze
A statement of ideas	argue, comment, state, establish, acknowledge, attribute, propose, observe, mention, identify, note, expand, emphasize, elaborate, stress
A description of data	define, signify, symbolize, acquire, impact, reflect, indicate, demonstrate, approximate

A statement of position	<ul><li>Positive: propose, hold the view that, hypothesize, advocate</li><li>Negative: negate, deny, reject, dispute</li></ul>
A demonstration of uncertainty	speculate, imply, predict, expect, project
A demonstration of components	consist, include, incorporate, comprise

These verbs can be used in any academic paper about any subject.

The Alternatives of Common Verbs

As was stated before, it is possible to use common simple, colloquial verbs in academic papers. However, an appliance of more official alternatives demonstrates higher knowledge of a student. The table below presents common verbs and synonyms that can be used instead:

Common Verb Phrases	Alternative Verbs
To find out about	see, learn, search, inquire, inspect, explore, investigate, detect, identify, uncover, assess, analyze, calculate, check, determine, define
To test	inform, confirm, verify, establish, discern, falsify, ensure, substantiate
To look at	view, observe, review, approach become aware of, regard, perceive, study
To compare	match, contrast, relate, associate, correlate, distinguish, differentiate
To balance	consider, concede, evaluate, defend, speculate, acknowledge, decide, conclude, advocate
To show	demonstrate, suggest, illustrate, indicate, disclose,

	point out, make evident, testify, define, interpret, exemplify, comment on, affirm, assert
To decrease	degrade, reduce, depress, impair, weaken, restrict, limit, minimize, diminish, cut, drop, lessen, moderate
To increase	advance, rise, elevate, arouse, enhance, enlarge, strengthen, excite, enrich, provoke, magnify, intensify
To answer	respond, reply
To give	furnish, provide, supply

Multiple Meanings of Phrasal Verbs

Many phrasal verbs have several meanings. In order to apply them correctly, it is important to know their descriptions. Some popular English phrasal verbs and their definitions are listed below.

1. **Break off** – to end something, or to stop doing something.
   - *The cooperation will go on until the members break off.*
   - *The correlation between these two elements finally broke off.*

2. **Turn around** – to change a direction, or to improve something.
   - *They turned around the direction of their research from focusing on psychological issues to chemical features of a human brain.*
   - *With the help of foreign experts, local authorities turned their unsuccessful business around.*

3. **Cut out** – to form something by cutting, or to remove.
   - *They cut out special overalls so employees can wear them while working.*
   - *Taylor (2016) cut out some contradictory findings from two previous studies.*

4. **Give away** – to betray or make known the notion of, or to give something as a present.
   - *The initial method of the research was given away before the better one was established.*
   - *Authorities gave away a big territory for building a new factory on it.*

It is significant to remember that verbs like break, turn, and cut have many other meanings. Their usage has to be coordinated with the context. Best of all is to refer to a dictionary.

Reporting Verbs

When we were talking about a narrative section of an essay, we stated that it is usually done in a form of reported speech. It, in turn, contains reporting verbs. They indicate that something was said by a particular person or source. What is more, a careful usage of reporting verbs shows how a writer understands the material. With the help of these kinds of verbs, it is possible to:

- Define whether someone's argument is correct or not.
- Express a neutral position concerning someone's argument.
- State that someone's argument is incorrect.

Look at the table below:

	A Positive Attitude	A Neutral Attitude	A Negative Attitude
Believing	guarantees, insists, asserts	claims, declares, expresses, thinks, maintains, believes, feels, holds, knows	hopes, imagines, guesses
Persuasion	argues, convinces, proves, promises, persuades, emphasizes, insists	encourages, reasons, justifies, assures	apologizes
Conclusion		realizes, finds, discovers, concludes	
Disagreement	accuses, complains, rejects, negates, disputes, disregards, rejects, contradicts, refuses, opposes, dismisses	requests, wonders, debates, questions, challenges	questions, hesitates
Presentation	promises	describes, defines, estimates, reports, studies, uses, talks,	confuses

		lists, implies, illustrates, identifies, observes, reminds	
Suggestion	recommends	advocates, proposes, theorizes, suggests, postulates	intimates, speculates

All in all, in academic writing verbs are as important as the substantives to which they are related. A correct usage of verbs makes an essay smooth, easy to read, and logically adjusted.

Works Cited

Curtin University. "Verb Tenses and Purpose." *curtin.edu.au*, studyskills.curtin.edu.au/good-grammar/section-1-verbs-in-academic-writing/verb-tenses-and-purpose/. Accessed 4 Sept. 2017.

Khoo, Elaine. "Verbs in Academic Writing." *University of Toronto at Scarborough*, utsc.utoronto.ca/twc/sites/utsc.utoronto.ca.twc/files/resource-files/xVerbs.pdf. Accessed 4 Sept. 2017.

My English Teacher. "10 Commonly Used Multiple Meaning Phrasal Verbs in English." *myenglishteacher.eu*, myenglishteacher.eu/blog/most-commonly-used-multiple-meanings-phrasal-verbs-in-english/. Accessed 4 Sept. 2017.

Norris, Carolyn Brimley. "Academic Writing in English." *University of Helsinki*, helsinki.fi/kksc/language.services/AcadWrit.pdf. Accessed 4 Sept. 2017.

University of Technology Sydney. "Reporting Verbs." *uts.edu.au*, uts.edu.au/sites/default/files/Reporting%20Verbs%20Reference%20Sheet.pdf. Accessed 5 Sept. 2017.

3.4. Phrases to Use in Academic Writing

In order to write a good academic paper, it is not enough to examine only the subject of your discussion. Good ideas and valid supportive arguments are essential, but it is also important to know how to present the material. Special phrases help with that.

There are expressions that can be applied to all disciplines. They allow readers to recognize an academic style of narration from others writing tomes. Academic phrases are conventional, so they help to avoid the confusing situation when an audience comes across unknown or unsuitable expressions. Since each particular section of an academic essay demands different phrases, our lists are organized according to the order of narration.

Phrases for Describing Research

This is the first section of an academic essay. Before a research is started, it has to be described. Specifically, an author should answer why a chosen subject is significant and what new aspects readers will know from the work. It is also important to notice that an over-explanation is just as bad as an under-explanation. It is significant to maintain a balance in writing. It is helpful to describe a research problem from four different sides:

Functions	Examples
Phrases that indicate why a subject (X) is important.	• It is common knowledge / generally known / well accepted that X is … • X is a critical / helpful / common part of … • X has many adaptations / implications / roles in the field of … • X is the major / main / primary / leading cause of … • X is responsible for … • X is believed to be / widely considered to be / recognized as the most important … • X is set to become a vital factor in … • A useful / remarkable / noticeable feature of X is that … • The major / fundamental / principal characteristics of X are … • X is undergoing a transformation in terms of … • X is attracting significant / increasing / noticeable interest due to …
Phrases that present background information concerning X (without direct references to the literature).	• The first / Initial / Preliminary studies of X considered it to be … • Traditionally X has always been viewed as … • X has received much attention in the past decade / over the last two decades / in the last two years … • Recent findings regarding / Developments in X have led to … • X has become an important / a central / a critical issue in … • Until now / For many years X has been considered as … • The last century X was viewed as / considered

	to be / seen as the most … • Experts / Scientists / Researchers have always seen X as …
Phrases that indicate the possible future for X.	• In the next few years, X is likely to have become / will become … • Within the next few years, X is likely / set / destined to become a significant component in … • X will shortly / soon / inevitably / rapidly be an issue that … • Within the next several years, X will become …
Phrases that indicate the gap in knowledge about X or possible limitations.	• The core / central problem of X is … • A common / major / basic / crucial / fundamental issue of X is … • Current solutions to X are incorrect / inadequate / inefficient / inconsistent / ineffective / unsatisfactory because … • It is not yet known whether X is … • X is often impractical / not feasible because of … • X is still not widely explained. • One of the main problems in the understanding of X is a lack of … • A major difficulty / disadvantage of X is … • An intriguing / important / challenging / neglected area in the field of X is … • Nevertheless, there is still a need for discussion concerning X … • Many hypotheses regarding X seem to be not well grounded / questionable / unfounded / disputable /unsupported / debatable. • The characteristics of X are not well understood.

	<ul><li>What is more, other approaches / solutions / research findings have failed to provide …</li><li>Most studies have only focused on …</li><li>There is no general agreement on …</li><li>Recent work has only focused on / failed to address …</li><li>Few researchers have addressed the question / problem / issue of …</li><li>The community has raised some issues about X concerning …</li></ul>

Phrases for Stating Your Aims

After the background information concerning a subject of interest was presented, an author should state the aims of this particular study. It is useful to do that with the following phrases:

- In this study / research / trial / report / review we …
- This study / research / trial / report / review present / proposes / describes new ideas concerning …
- This paper examines / observes / investigates / discusses how to solve …
- This study is a report on …
- X is observed / discussed / presented with an aim to …
- The aim of this work is to give additional knowledge concerning …
- The present knowledge of X is not enough. The goal of this paper is to extend current data concerning …
- The aim of the study is to validate / examine / determine / analyze / calculate / estimate …
- In the present context, X can be further discussed as …
- We believe that we have found a significant solution concerning …
- The paper takes a look at / calls into question / re-examines …
- This paper attempts to show that …
- The central thesis of this paper is that …
- This paper contests the claim that …
- This paper examines the importance of X in the aspect of …

- In the pages that follow, it will be argued that …

- Further discussion will show that …

- This paper investigates the usefulness of …

Phrases for Referencing

After the background information is given and aims of the present research are established, we go to the main body of the paper.

As was discussed in previous chapters of our guidebook, this section presents writers' ideas which have to be supported by arguments from valid studies. In such a way, it is important to know how to incorporate citations and paraphrasing into an essay. These phrases will help to do this process correctly:

- According to previous studies, …

- Recent works have suggested that …

- There is some evidence that suggest that …

- Previous trials have reported that …

- According to Taylor, …

- According to recent reports / studies / findings …

- According to many in the field …

- Taylor (2016) holds the view that …

- Taylor's (2016) study is accurate …

- Many researchers hold the view / believe that …

- Research conducted by Taylor (2016) shows that …

- As Taylor (2016) suggested, …

- A few studies concerning X have reported …

- The first serious discussion in reference to X appeared in …

- It is thought that …

- It is suggested that …

- It is believed that …

- It is widely known that …

- It has been reported that …

- It has been widely assumed that …

Phrases for Analyzing Data

There are also phrases that can help to introduce findings of the present research. Examples are listed below:

Functions of Phrases	Examples
Indicating positive results	<ul><li>On average, X was shown to have …</li><li>Strong evidence of X was found when …</li><li>A significant positive correlation was found between …</li><li>Further investigation showed that …</li><li>The mean score for X was …</li><li>A positive correlation was found between X and …</li><li>The findings, as shown in Table 1, suggest that …</li><li>There was an important difference between the two aspects / factors …</li></ul>
Indicating negative results	<ul><li>There were no important differences between …</li><li>No important differences were found between …</li><li>No changes in X were noticed …</li><li>None of these differences were statistically important.</li></ul>
Indicating interesting / helpful results	<ul><li>Interestingly, this correlation is related to …</li><li>The most surprising interrelation is with the …</li><li>The most surprising aspect of the trial is in the …</li><li>The connectivity between X and Y is interesting due to the fact that …</li><li>The most important finding showed that …</li></ul>

Indicating problematic results	<ul><li>A possible explanation concerning this may be that …</li><li>It appears that these results are due to …</li><li>The observed change in X could be linked to …</li><li>This contradictory result may happen due to …</li><li>There are few possible reasons for this result.</li><li>There are several likely causes for such a controversial result.</li><li>This unbalance could be attributed to …</li><li>This lack of agreement may be due to …</li><li>The findings must be interpreted with caution because …</li></ul>

All mentioned phrases give an essay a pleasant academic appearance. They help to introduce material and make writing smooth and logical. However, be sure that you do not overuse academic expressions. A moderate amount of them in suitable places of your writing is good. On the other hand, too many phrases make the work scratchy and far fetched, and complicate the reading.

Works Cited

Manchester 1824. "Academic Phrasebank." *manchester.ac.uk*, phrasebank.manchester.ac.uk/using-cautious-language/. Accessed 1 Sept. 2017.

Morley, John. "Academic Phrasebank." *googleusercontent.com*, kfs.edu.eg/com/pdf/2082015294739.pdf. Accessed 1 Sept. 2017.

My English Teacher.eu. "Essential Academic Writing Examples and Phrases!" *myenglishteacher.eu*, myenglishteacher.eu/blog/academic-writing-examples-and-phrases/. Accessed 1 Sept. 2017.

Springer. "English for Writing Research Papers. Useful Phrases." *springer.com*, springer.com/cda/content/document/cda_downloaddocument/Free+Download+-+Useful+Phrases.pdf?SGWID=0-0-45-1543172-p177775190. Accessed 1 Sept. 2017.

3.5. Commonly Confused Words in Academic Writing

The English language is a well-built system of linguistic units. However, it contains some ambiguous issues that can be confusing for both native and non-native speakers. Due to the fact that many students refer to English as the language of their studies, it is important for them to know its peculiarities. Specifically, it has many pairs of words that sound alike but have different meanings or sound differently but name the same notion. This chapter of our guide will describe commonly confused English words that are widely used in academic writing.

Homonyms

Homonyms make the first group of possibly confused words. A **homonym** is a word which is said or spelled similarly as another word but has a completely different meaning.

For examples look at the table below:

Homonyms	Definitions	Examples
Address	1. (verb) to speak to (someone); to refer to (something). 2. (noun) a location.	• In this research paper, we **address** the issue of the effectiveness of a laser spine surgery. • If you have more questions, feel free to send letters to the **address** that is given

		below.
Band	1. (noun) a musical group. 2. (verb) to tie.	• The **band** will start their world tour in December 2017. • Boxes were **banded** with iron rings.
Current	1. (adjective) up to date; happening now. 2. (noun) a flow of water.	• A **current** study appears to be a prolongation of the previous one. • A powerful **current** of ocean water ruined the surrounding communities.
Kind	1. (noun) a type. 2. (adjective) caring.	• This was the error of the first **kind**. • We appreciate your **kind** answer in advance.
Lie	1. (verb) to lean back. 2. (verb) to tell a falsehood.	• Results of the research **lie** within the experiment. • Unfortunately, readers believed in a **lie** from journalists and the rebellion began.
Match	1. (verb) to pair some items. 2. (noun) a stick for making a fire.	• All participants were **matched** according to their ages. • Do not strike **matches** in this building. Its walls are inflammable.
Mean	1. (adjective) average. 2. (adjective) not nice.	• The daily **mean** of this quantity comes down to four. • The lady complained to the jury about the **mean** look of her boss.
Tender	1. (adjective) gentle; sensitive; painful. 2. (verb) to pay money; to propose a payment.	• The study analyzed ten patients with the **tender** abdomen. • Authorities of one state **tendered** a price for their products to the government of the country.
Tire	1. (verb) to exhaust.	• The trial **tired** all participants.

	2. (noun) a part of a wheel.	• Do not forget to put the **tire** on the wheel before driving.

Homophones

Homophones make the second group of possibly confused words. A *homophone* is a word that sounds alike with another word but has a different spelling and meaning.

For examples look at the table below:

Homophones	Definitions	Examples
1) *Affect* 2) *Effect*	1) To influence something; to change. 2) (verb) to make something happen; to implement; to perform. (noun) A consequence of something.	- The new medicine **affected** the patients in a bad way. - Human activity **affects** the environment. - The governor **effected** many laws in his state. - The side-**effect** of this drug boils down to constipation and insomnia.
1) *Accept* 2) *Except*	1) To trust; to agree; to embrace; to take. 2) Apart from (something).	- Many contemporary researchers **accepted** this theory that was made fifty years ago as a valid one. - All symptoms of a patient **except** his urinary problems point out that he has Cervical Spinal Stenosis.
1) *Their* 2) *There* 3) *They're*	1) (adjective) belonging to. 2) (adverb) refers to a place. 3) Contraction of *they are*. *Note:* In academic writing it is not advisable to make contractions. It is recommended to write *they are, we are*, and *you will* instead of *they're, we're*, and	- **Their** study will be published the next year. - **There** you can find more examples of commonly confused words.

	you'll.	
1) To *2) Too* *3) Two*	1) It is a preposition. 2) It is an adverb that means also, in addition. 3) A numeral.	- **To** test this drug, experts have chosen ten participants. - The results of this conference will be stated **too**. - **Two** groups of children took part in the experiment.
1) Then *2) Than*	At that time. Used in a comparison of two or more notions.	- Try to do this exercise for a month. **Then**, write me concerning improvements or declines. - This new book seems to be more helpful **than** the other one written two years ago.
1) Where *2) Wear*	(adverb) refers to a place. (verb) to carry clothes.	- No one knew **where** the treasures have gone. - It is important for a nurse to **wear** sterile gloves while dealing with patients.
1) Brake *2) Break*	To slow down. To smash.	- Before the movement began, they checked the **brake** system of their car. - The glass was **broken** and all liquid was spread over the surface.
1) Hardy *2) Hearty*	(adjective) strong. (adjective) genuine.	- This glass is winter-**hardy** so it is possible to fix it on a porch. - His poems are still estimated as the best **hearty** creations of the 19th century.
1) Hole *2) Whole*	(noun) an opening. (adjective) complete.	- The **hole** in the wall makes the audibility too high. - The **whole** city was celebrating

		the national festival.
1) All ready *2) Already*	Means that everything is prepared. By this time.	- **All** my essays were **ready** by Sunday night. - I have **already** sent my essays to the professor.
1) Presence *2) Presents*	A present state. Gifts.	- His **presence** in the meeting made everyone surprised. - All participants received **presents** by the end of the experiment.
1) Principal *2)Principle*	1) The head of a school. 2) A law.	- The **Principal** approved new changes in the learning system of the school. - The main **principle** of this University is to encourage students to be creative in their academic work.

Apostrophes

Apostrophes are used to show possession. In order to write them correctly, refer to the table below:

Purpose of Usage	Examples
To show a possession with a singular noun.	- A **student's** essay. - A **professor's** recommendations. - A **librarian's** advice.
To show a possession to a proper noun that ends with **s.**	- Mrs. **Jones'** tea party. - **Texas'** hurricane.
To show a possession to plural nouns that end with **s.**	- The **guys'** club. - **Letters'** stamps. - **Researchers'** verdicts.

To show a possession to nouns that have a plural form initially.	- The **children's** hour. - The **teeth's** problems.
To show a possession to compound nouns.	- A **mother-in-law's** opinion.
To show a possession to two people who share the same item.	- **Taylor and Young's** examination appeared to be the most successful among others. - **Her and Taylor's** book.
If you need to emphasize on a separation, put 's after both names.	- **Taylor's and Young's** studies are both valid enough.

Other Examples

There are words that do not sound alike and do not have a similar spelling but are still used incorrectly in academic writing.

Although – While

Although (conjunction): indicates a contrast.

> **Although** laser spinal surgery may have some benefits, its effectiveness is rather exaggerated.

While (conjunction): indicates a time period of something. Can be also used as a noun.

> **While** patients were sleeping, the drug was functioning and experts were making notes.

Because – Since

Because (conjunction): shows causation.

> They want to make this trial **because** they are interested in results.

Since (can be used as preposition/conjunction/adverb): refers to the time of something.

> The participants have not been home **since** the examination began.

If – Whether

If (conjunction): explains an effect or consequence of something that happens or is true.

> **If** a new vaccine appears to be helpful, the production of it will grow.

Whether (pronoun): refers to options between alternatives.

> **Whether** a new vaccine appears to be helpful or not, its production will grow anyway.

Historic – Historical

Historic: important, famous, affluent.

Authorities made renovation activities in the park where Lincoln made his **historic** speech concerning the American Civil War.

Historical: related to history.

Historical belongings are saved in the museum.

Learned – Learnt

Learned is an American past tense form of the verb *learn*.

Learnt is the same, but used in British English.

Gray – Grey

Gray is the name of a color between black and white, typed in American spelling norms.

Grey is the same word but spelled in the most common form in British English.

Defence – Defense

Defence is written in British English spelling norms.

Defense is the common spelling for the American variant of the same word.

Among – Amongst

Among and *amongst* are variants of the same word, though *amongst* is considered more rare, particularly so in American English.

Farther – Further

Farther indicates a physical distance.

Sean can jump **farther** than Kelly.

Further indicates an imaginary (metaphorical) distance.

Sean is **further** away from writing his essay than Kelly is.

Advice – Advise

Advice is a noun.

She received good **advice** from her teacher.

Advise is a verb.

Her teacher **advised** her to focus on the poetry instead of the prose.

Complement – Compliment

Complement is something which completes something else; it gives additional details or qualities.

Such questions will be a great **complement** to this research.

A *compliment* is a saying that consists of pleasant words.

The doctor received many **compliments** after the successful surgery.

Among – Between

The adverb *among* is used when we need to indicate several items.

He was searching for this file **among** others on the desk.

The adverb *between* is applied when we point on two items.

The **difference** between Taylor's and Young's studies boils down to diverse control groups.

The appliance of commonly confused words requires knowledge. A student needs to be fully aware of every lexical unit he or she uses. In order to avoid mistakes, it is recommended to always check the work several times. Refer to our guide to make your writing easier.

Works Cited

Enago Academy. "Word Choice in Academic Writing: Commonly Confused English Words." *enago.com*, enago.com/academy/commonly-confused-english-words/. Accessed 17 Sept. 2017.

GrammarBook.com. "Apostrophes." *grammarbook.com*, grammarbook.com/punctuation/apostro.asp. Accessed 17 Sept. 2017.

Grammarly Blog. "Top 30 Commonly Confused Words in English." *grammarly.com*, grammarly.com/blog/commonly-confused-words/. Accessed 17 Sept. 2017.

HuffPost. "Commonly Confused Words: How to Avoid These Grammar Gaffes." *huffingtonpost.com*, huffingtonpost.com/2015/02/04/commonly-confused-words_n_6599214.html. Accessed 17 Sept. 2017.

Monmouth University. "Homonyms." *monmouth.edu*, monmouth.edu/uploadedFiles/Resources_for_Writers/Grammar_and_Punctuation/Homonyms.pdf. Accessed 17 Sept. 2017.

Singularis Ltd. "Homophones." *singularis.ltd.uk*, singularis.ltd.uk/bifroest/misc/homophones-list.html. Accessed 18 Sept. 2017.

Vocabulary.com. "Homonym/Homophone/Homograph." *vocabulary.com*, vocabulary.com/articles/chooseyourwords/homonym-homophone-homograph/. Accessed 17 Sept. 2017.

Your Dictionary. "Examples of Homonyms." *yourdictionary.com*, examples.yourdictionary.com/examples-of-homonyms.html. Accessed 17 Sept. 2017.

Chapter 4. Formatting Styles

Academic writing is performed with the help of different formatting styles. These styles help to build a strong system for scholarly work, which includes the author's analysis of valid sources and opinion towards a subject of interest. According to the different formatting styles, the execution of documents is different.

In the following chapter of our guide, you will find out about the main formats of academic writing:

- MLA
- APA
- Chicago/Turabian
- Harvard

These formatting styles are given in comparison, so you will be able to learn:

- Types of scholarly disciplines that refer to each style.
- Peculiarities of these styles.
- Correct formatting of title pages.
- Correct in-text citations and referencing formats.
- Special aspects of in-text citations from different types of sources for each style.

A comparative analysis will show differences between all formats so that you can develop a clear understanding of how to complete school assignments of any format correctly. Follow our recommendations to become a master of academic writing and gain knowledge concerning all common formatting styles.

4.1. APA Formatting Style

APA style was developed by the American Psychological Association for academic institutions. It serves for creating collegiate papers with proper citation of scientific sources. Despite the fact that the style was produced by scholars who find their area of expertise in psychology, nowadays the APA format is used by various researchers to write about diverse academic issues. Apart from this style, there are also MLA and Chicago formatting styles of writing, but APA appears to be the most popular for scientific fields.

The latest Publication Manual that the American Psychological Association published recently is in the 6th edition. Here authors give detailed descriptions of the structure of papers, appropriate grammar patterns, and correct citations.

The APA style of writing is known for its strong feature set. As for a general text appearance, papers in this format are always typed in 12 pt., Times New Roman font, double-spaced, and have one-inch margins on all sides.

As for the number of components, they consist of:

- A **page header** (also named as a **running head**) which is placed at the top of every page. It is typed in capital letters. The page header is a shortened version of the title of the paper and can contain no more than 50 characters (spacing and punctuation are included in this number); numbers of pages stand on the right top corner of the page.
  RUNNING HEAD: TITLE OF THE PAPER   1

- A **title page** which includes the title of the paper, the author's name, and the name of the institution where the paper was created.

    On the title page the running head has this form:

    RUNNING HEAD: TITLE OF THE PAPER

    On other pages it is done in this way:

    TITLE OF THE PAPER

    The title in the center is typed in the standard way, using standard title case. It is centered on the page and positioned a third of the way down the page. It is suggested that the title has no more than 12 words and contains no abbreviations or unnecessary dictionary terms. All in all, the title can take up to two lines. Text on all pages, as well as on the title page, has to be double-spaced.

    After the title of the paper goes the author's name. It typically includes the first name, initials of the middle name, and the last name without any other titles or degrees (such as Dr. or PhD). Then the institutional affiliation is stated. It indicates the place where the paper was developed.

- An **abstract** that is a summary of the key points of the made research. It begins with the new page which also has the page header and the page number above. The first line of the abstract page contains the word "Abstract" typed in a standard method (no italics, formatting, quotation marks, or bold font). The abstract itself consists of 150-250 words and includes everything concerning the made research: a topic, questions, methods, participants, analysis of data, results, conclusions, and a further discussion. It is also possible to state suggestions for future work and keywords of the paper (the word "Keywords" is italicized).

    Keywords: diabetes, obesity, cancer, cardiac failure…

    A list of keywords can help other researchers to find the paper in databases. All in all, the abstract is written as one paragraph, also double-spaced. Keywords are typed separately, as the next paragraph.

- The **main body** is an another major component of an essay written in APA style. Its structure depends on the type of paper (research papers, expository essays, or rhetorical analyses are done according to different schemes). In all accounts, the main body is written in an academic style of writing, typed in 12 pt. Times New Roman font, and its lines are double spaced. There can be an unlimited number of paragraphs which logically coincide one with another.

- **References** form the final part of the APA style paper. They consist of works that were used during the preparation of the essay.

In-Text Citations with Examples

In-text citations refer to experts whose works are relevant for the present research. In order to state their names and impacts, the past or present perfect tenses are used:

Taylor (2017) admitted that …

Taylor (2017) has admitted that …

As we can see, APA style follows a name-date method of citation (name + date of the targeted finding). In writing, after a particular citation from a previously-made research is used, it is followed by parentheses containing the citation information:

(Taylor, 2017).

A complete reference to this researcher and the publication should be stated in the References section. Proper nouns (names, initials) are always capitalized:

D. Taylor.

If a name of a source is mentioned, all words in the source (except conjunctions between them) are also capitalized:

War and Peace.

New Century World.

Now or Never.

In the References section, only the first word of a title is capitalized (and the following first word after a colon, and proper nouns inside the title):

War and peace.

Certain works that are considered standalone should be italicized or underlined (titles of books, movies, television series, or song titles). In most cases, these works will be italicized (unless the paper is handwritten):

A Walk to Remember.

<u>Rebel Without a Cause</u>.

The World According to Garp.

If a work is part of a greater body of work, it should be put into quotation marks (titles of articles, television episodes, song titles, or blog posts):

"As long as we are in love."

"Castle."

"16 features of hypersensitive people."

If the quote is taken exclusively from the work, it should be accompanied by the author, year of publication, and in the References also will be listed the page number where it was taken.

According to Taylor, "classic American cinematography includes more artistic work than contemporary movies and cartoons" (2017).

Taylor suggested that classic American cinematography includes more artistic work than contemporary movies and cartoons (Taylor, 2017).

If quotations are long (more than 40 words), they should be put in a separately standing block of typed lines without quotation marks. The quotation begins with a new line (as a new paragraph). In addition to this, double-spacing and 1/2 inch from the left margin are maintained throughout the whole quotation.

Taylor's research (2017) found the following:

> Contemporary American cartoons and movies are made with the help of the latest media technologies and abilities. Because of an opportunity to shoot films on digital devices and later put in music recordings or voice work on them, the process of movie making became relatively different. In such a way, it is fair to admit that it was transformed from a work of art into a computerized process. Consequently, nowadays, it is not enough for an artist to simply draw. He has to know programming codes, or he will not be in demand for film studios.

If quotations are paraphrased from an initial work, it is possible to use references only to the name of the author and the year of publication.

> According to Taylor, the process of movie making became relatively different due to an opportunity to shoot films with the help of the latest media technologies and abilities (2017).

References with Examples

A reference list ends the paper. It gives information about sources that were used and places where they can be found. Each source has to be sited separately. References are put on a freestanding page and titled with "References" at the top center of the page (the word is not underlined, not bolded, and without quotation marks). References are also typed in double-spaced format.

All lines begin flush with the left margin, with subsequent lines in each entry indented a half-inch from the left margin.

Clement, Brian. (2012). Scary sweets: The dangers of sugar. *One Green Planet*. Retrieved from http://www.onegreenplanet.org/foodandhealth/scary-sweets-the-dangers-of-sugar/

Cohen, Rich. (2013). "Sugar. A not so sweet story." *National Geographic*. Retrieved from http://ngm.nationalgeographic.com/2013/08/sugar/cohen-text

The last name of an author goes before the first name.

If a source has more than seven authors, the first six are listed, ellipses are put after them, and then the last author is stated.

> Just, Beth Haenke, Marc, David, Munns, Megan, Taylor, John, Young, Kelly, Murphy, Brooke, … & Sandefer, Ryan. (2016). Why patient matching is a challenge: Research on master patient index (MPI) data discrepancies in key identifying fields. *Perspectives in Health Information Management.* Retrieved from http://perspectives.ahima.org/why-patient-matching-is-a-challenge-research-on-master-patient-index-mpi-data-discrepancies-in-key-identifying-fields/

The basic form for a reference to an article from a periodical:

> Author, A. A., Author, B. B., & Author, C. C. (Year). The title of article. *The title of Periodical, volume number* (issue number), pages. http://dx.doi.org/xx.xxx/yyyyy

The basic form for a reference to a book:

> Author, A. A. (Year of publication). *The title of work: Capital letter also for subtitle.* Location: Publisher.

The basic form for a reference from an electronic source:

> Author, A. A., & Author, B. B. (Date of publication). The title of article. *The title of Online Periodical, volume number* (issue number if available). Retrieved from http://www.bbc.com/news/health-26448399

Some extra points to follow:

- References should be alphabetized.
- Journal titles should be written in full.
- All main words in journal titles have to be capitalized.
- In references to books, articles, and web pages, the first letter of the first word of a title should be capitalized, the rest in lower case (except for proper nouns).

APA style is a popular format for writing academic papers on various topics. It is notable for its clearness, precision, and ease. The style is commonly used in psychology studies as well as in other scientific branches.

Works Cited

American Psychological Association. "APA Style." *apastyle.org*,
     www.apastyle.org/learn/index.aspx. Accessed 3 Aug. 2017.

American Psychological Association. "APA Style CENTRAL." *apastyle.org*,
     www.apastyle.org/index.aspx. Accessed 3 Aug. 2017.

Bibme. "Your Ultimate APA Format Guide & Generator." *bibme.org*, www.bibme.org/apa.
     Accessed 4 Aug. 2017.

The Purdue Online Writing Lab. "APA Style." *purdue.edu*,
     owl.english.purdue.edu/owl/section/2/10/. Accessed 5 Aug. 2017.

4.2. MLA Formatting Style

The Modern Language Association (MLA) style is widely used in academic writing concerning the subjects of art, literature, and human sciences.

In the past half of the century, MLA was adopted as one of the leading styles for scholarly writing. It is often used by publishers, researchers, members of the press, and, of course, students. In order to make the style as useful as possible, experts described it in several basic rules instead of specific principles. For instance, MLA has strongly developed standards of citations which can be used for any source that needs to be mentioned. In such a way, the style is flexible. Once users learn its regulations, they can apply them to any academic work they need to complete, regardless of the field, genre, type of sources, or type of paper an assignment demands.

Two core elements of MLA style are in-text citations and the Works Cited page, where used sources are mentioned in necessary detail.

In-Text Citations with Examples

MLA style demands a parenthetical citation of reference links. This means that relevant information about a source is placed in parentheses after a quotation or a paraphrase. It is important to remember that any resource that is used in the text of an academic work has to be then mentioned in the Works Cited section.

Author-Page Format

In-text citations are always done in this format. Specifically, the last name of the author and the page number on which the author's words were placed in the initial source have to be in parentheses. A complete reference to this author and the resource must appear in the Works Cited section. It is possible to incorporate the name of the writer in the sentence or mention the name only after the sentence. The number of the page, in its turn, always appears only in parentheses, if available. Compare:

> His best aim is to set up a business which is why he contemplates concerning a "little liquor store" **(Hansberry 494)** that may help the Youngers to get rid of all their misfortunes.

> **As the author** admits, "After much wavering and vacillating, the Youngers decided to continue with their plans to move in spite of their financial reversals and in spite of their having been warned by a weak representative of the white neighborhood that blacks are not welcome" **(James 4).**

In the first example, a citation is just incorporated in the text of the essay. It is followed by parentheses where the name of the author and the number of the page is presented. Interestingly, after that, the sentence goes on. The second example illustrates how it is possible to explicitly refer to a particular author and then also state information concerning the work in parentheses. What is more, it is also possible to write it like this:

> On this occasion, **Brooks** comments: "America is especially sensitive to war weariness, and nothing brings on a backlash like the perception of defeat. I say 'perception' because America is a very all-or-nothing society. We like the big win, the touchdown, the knockout in the first round. We like to know, and for everyone else to know, that our victory wasn't only uncontested, it was positively devastating" **(53-54).**

Only the pages of the source text go in parentheses because the author was already mentioned in the text itself. If they want more information about the resource, they can go to the Works Cited page and find it under the name "Brooks." For example:

Brooks, Max. *World War Z: An Oral History of the Zombie War.* Crown Publishing Group, 2006.

In-Text Citations for Print Resources (Author Is Known)

Sources included: academic journal articles, books, newspapers, magazines.

For any of these resources, give the author's last name and the page number (when applicable). As was stated before, if the name of an author is mentioned in the sentence with a citation, there is no need to repeat it in the parentheses. See the following:

Strong people have been described by **Sean Taylor** as "those who can overcome anything by remaining faithful to moral virtues" (**4**).

Strong people have been defined as "those who can overcome anything by remaining faithful to moral virtues" (**Taylor 4**).

These examples have to correspond to a name of a source that begins with Taylor in the Works Cited section:

Taylor, Sean. *Human Virtues and Vices: what people choose when their lives fall apart.* Los Angeles: U of California, 2016.

In-Text Citations for Print Resources (Collective Author)

When the source was written by a corporate author, an in-text citation is made from the name of this corporation and the page number where the citation is placed. It is also acceptable to use abbreviations in order to avoid lengthy parenthetical citations. For example, "national" can be shortened into "nat'l":

As it was stated, "the result was accepted by last year's conference in Paris" (**Nat'l** Group of Modern Scientists 265).

In-Text Citations for Print Resources (Unknown Author)

If an author of a source is not known, it is acceptable to use a shorter name for the work. For instance, when this work is not big (like an article), put the name in quotation marks. If the work is a self-contained work (books, names of websites, shows, films), italicize its name and give a page number as usual.

Many experts believe that depression is a mental disorder that can be controlled by the person who appears under its effects. Specifically, according to them, "depression is no more than a negative mindset that its owner chooses to be in. Consequently, the illness can be eliminated by changing mental patterns of the individual. Despite the fact that there are people who are more prone to getting depression than others, almost every person can overcome this disease by controlling his thinking" (**"The Cause-Effective Relationship of Mental Disorders" 10**).

In this example, since readers do not know the author of the article, a shortened title of it is placed in the parenthetical citation. It corresponds to the full name of the article that is mentioned in the Works Cited section. In such a way, a writer of an academic work helps readers to find this source on the Work Cited page. It will look like this:

"The Cause-Effective Relationship of Mental Disorders and Easy-To-Understand
Treatments." *Mental Health: Be Aware,* 2016, www.thenameofthesite.org/.
11 Sept. 2017.

Author-Page Citations for Literary Works with Several Editions

Along with the author's name and page number, it is sometimes useful to give more information about a source itself. This holds especially true if it has multiple editions. It is impossible to predict which editions readers have. As a result, it is better to point to a version that was used in this particular academic work. Additional information may include:

- book (bk.);
- section (sec.);
- part (pt.);
- volume (vol.);
- chapter (ch.);
- paragraph (par.).

An example:

Lord Byron developed many poetry samples on the theme of love (45; ch. 3).

Authors with Same Last Names

In this case, it is acceptable to give initials of first names of authors.

Although many experts admit that the production of fast food negatively affects the environment (**S. Taylor** 23), others state that the conditions of nature can withstand it (**K. Taylor** 16).

A source with several authors.

If a source was made by two writers, state their last names in your writing or in a parenthetical citation:

Taylor and **Young** suggest that American classical movies were shot on excellent cameras, so they have not lost their quality over time (**16**).

The experts state that American classical movies remain of first-rate quality nowadays, which means that they "were shot on excellent cameras" (**Taylor and Young 16**).

A work cited entry will look like this:

Taylor, Sean, and Kelly Young. "American Classical Movies: Their Value in the Present-Day Movie World." *American History in Ten Words*, vol. 248, no. 2, Fall 2015, pp. 9-26.

If a source was made by more than two authors, state only the last name of the first writer and replace all other names with "et al."

According to **Young et al.**, "American classical movies held more meaning than modern films where it is immensely replaced by visual effects" (94).

The authors admit that moral duties are the same for the majority of citizens of the world, despite their religions, cultures, and places of origin (**Young et al.** 57).

A work cited entry will look like this:

Young, Kelly, et al. "Current Issues in the Moral Aspect of Humanity." *American Journal*, vol. 78, no. 1, Jan. 2009, pp. 46-102.

Several Works by the Same Author

In this case, shortened titles of works should be mentioned together with page numbers. Shortened names of articles must be placed in quotation marks while book titles must be italicized. See the examples:

Although Jarred does not support the idea of using essential oils for people with an inclination to allergic reactions (**"Essential Warning"** 12), he admits that some samples can ease the inflammation very effectively (**"Essential Oils: Benefits and Recommendations"** 24).

Despite the fact that the expert names journaling as an effective practice against mental problems (Resst et al., *Be Aware* 78), he also finds it irritating and forced in some cases (*Dealing with Mental Block* 3).

Quoting Indirect Sources

If you cite information from a source that also has it as cited, use "qtd. in" to point out the source you took the phrase from:

Hackly admits that college years can be an ultimate experience to those "who do not exactly know where to apply personal energy and want to try different kinds of sport, meet new people, and learn more about themselves as well as about a chosen profession" (**qtd. in** Febber 90).

However, it is always better to find the initial resource and cite from it.

Non-Print Sources from the Internet

In-text citations of web sources need to include:

- The first word that is placed in the Works Cited section and corresponds to a quote (website title, author name, or article title).
- The website name should be partial (not the full URL).

There is no need to mention paragraph or page numbers of an internet source. Electronic sources may look like these:

The authors admit that moral duties are the same for the majority citizens of the world, despite their religions, cultures, and places of origin. (**Young et al.**).

One contemporary philosopher stated that strong people should be defined as "those who can overcome anything by remaining faithful to moral virtues" (**Taylor, "Human Virtues and Vices: What People Choose When Their Lives Fall Apart"**).

Work cited entries are like these:

Taylor, Sean. "Human Virtues and Vices: What People Choose When Their Lives Fall
  Apart." *UCLA*, 11 Sept. 2017, (the partial name of the electronic resource).

Young, Kelly, **et al.** "Current Issues in the Moral Aspect of Humanity." *American Journal*,
  11 Sept. 2017, (the partial name of the electronic resource).

Some citations are not needed. This is for facts which are considered common knowledge such as well-known quotations and proverbs. They can be used without stating their sources.

References with Examples

In MLA style, the Works Cited page is the end of the academic essay. All mentioned sources on it should correspond to those that were used in the main text. Here are some rules to consider:

- The Works Cited section should be placed on a separate page of a research paper and labeled "Works Cited" at the top of the page (without quotation marks, italics, or bold font).
- The header of this page is the same as on other pages. It includes the last name of the student and page number.
- The format of the Works Cited page is also double-spaced with one-inch margins.
- There should be no skipped lines between entries.
- To the second and following lines of each entry, 0.5 inches should be added to the margin.
- All sources (printed, electronic) should be properly cited.
- Online sources must include a location where they can be found. They can be written without the "https://" part of the address.
- Each entry begins with a new line.
- Every word in the name of a source begins with the capital letter (except for articles such as "the" and "an," prepositions, and conjunctions between main words).
- Titles of larger works (books, newspapers) are italicized, while names of shorter sources (articles, poems) are put in quotation marks.
- Author names are written in alphabetical order according to their last names. The correct order:

  Jarred, Samuel

Taylor, Sean A.

Young, Kelly.

Personal titles are not mentioned, as well as degrees.

- If there are several works by the same author listed, their titles are placed alphabetically. The second title follows three hyphens that replace the author's name.

    Taylor, Sean A. *The Grammar of American Classical Movies.* [...]

    ---. *The Scheme of Plot in American Classical Movies.* [...]

- If you have sources with unknown authors, alphabetize them too. They can be put between works of authors who are known.

    Jarred, Samuel. *Art of the Crime.* [...]

    Names of the Most Famous Detectives in the USA. [...]

    Taylor, Sean A. *The Grammar of American Classical Movies.* [...]

    Young, Kelly. "Current Issues in the Moral Aspect of Humanity." [...]

Follow this complete guide on MLA style of academic writing to develop credible, correctly established papers.

Works Cited

Modern Language Association. "MLA Style." *mla.org,* mla.org/MLA-Style. Accessed 11 Sept. 2017.

Purdue Online Writing Lab. "MLA Style." *purdue.edu,* owl.english.purdue.edu/owl/section/2/11/. Accessed 11 Sept. 2017.

4.3. Chicago/Turabian Formatting Style

Chicago/Turabian style of academic writing is widely used for creating manuscripts, publications, documents, researches, and essays concerning different scholarly subjects. It has two main aspects that boil down to:

- The Notes-Bibliography (NB) that is used in papers on history, the arts, and literature.

- The Author-Date System that is common for papers on social issues and sciences.

Our guide will focus on NB since it is more widespread among students' assignments. The NB system in Chicago Style allows writers to reference sources they use with the help of **footnote** and **endnote** citations, and a Bibliography section in the paper. What is more, writers can add personal comments concerning sources. The NB system also serves as a great protection against plagiarism because it demands a very precise use of footnotes and endnotes. When they are correct, the credibility of the paper becomes very high, which is obviously good for its author.

General Chicago/Turabian Style Features

There are several important peculiarities of the style that are necessary for every academic work written in it:

- Margins of paper can vary from 1 inch to 1.5 inches.

- The print should be easy to interpret. The most common font is Times New Roman.

- It is recommended to use a 12 pt. font size.

- The text is normally double-spaced. However:

- Titles of tables, quotations in blocks, and captions for figures/charts are single-spaced.

- Quotations from prose that take more than five lines should be placed in a block.

- Block quotes are indented half an inch as a unit.

- Block quotations are not placed in quotation marks.

- They are separated from the initial text by an extra line space.

Look at the example below:

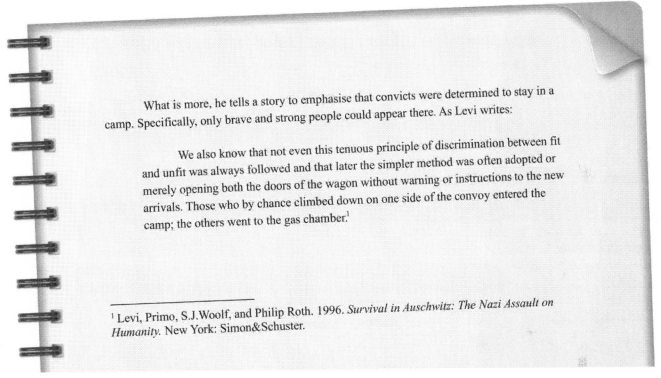

What is more, he tells a story to emphasise that convicts were determined to stay in a camp. Specifically, only brave and strong people could appear there. As Levi writes:

> We also know that not even this tenuous principle of discrimination between fit and unfit was always followed and that later the simpler method was often adopted or merely opening both the doors of the wagon without warning or instructions to the new arrivals. Those who by chance climbed down on one side of the convoy entered the camp; the others went to the gas chamber.[1]

---

[1] Levi, Primo, S.J.Woolf, and Philip Roth. 1996. *Survival in Auschwitz: The Nazi Assault on Humanity*. New York: Simon&Schuster.

- Bibliography and notes are also single-spaced. An extra line space between notes and bibliographic entries should be placed.

- Numbers of pages begin in the first page header.

- If a paper is rather long, a writer should use subheadings in it.

- It is advisable to apply an extra line before and after subheadings. No periods should be used.

Sections of the Paper

Title Page

- The title of work is centered and placed on the third part of the page from above.

- The student's name and information about his or her class are placed several lines below.

- If there is a subtitle, end the title with a colon and add them on the next line below the title.

Look at the example below:

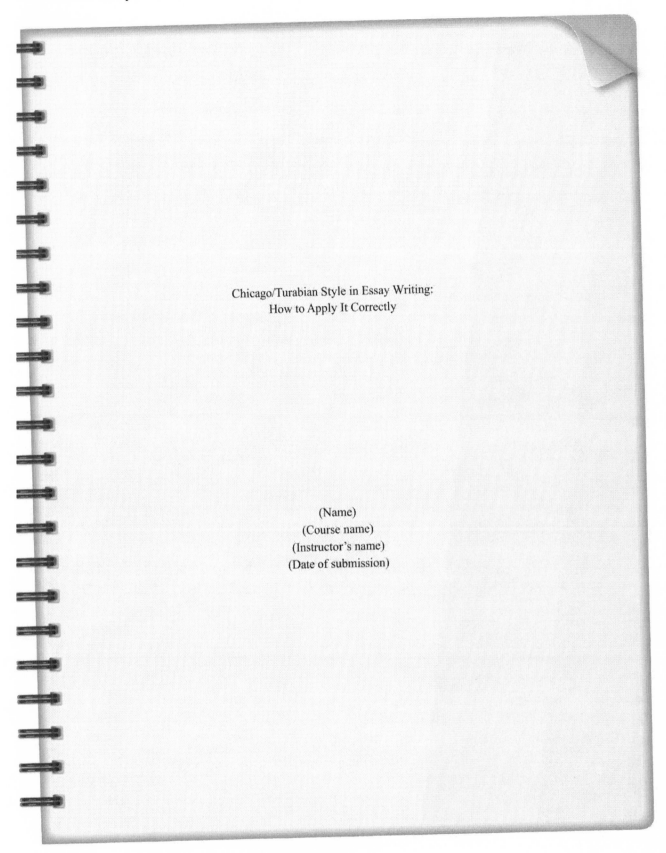

Chicago/Turabian Style in Essay Writing:
How to Apply It Correctly

(Name)
(Course name)
(Instructor's name)
(Date of submission)

Main Body

- All titles and subtitles that are used in the text, notes, and the bibliography should be capitalized.

- Titles and subtitles are normally placed in quotation marks. However:

  - Names of larger works (such as books, periodicals, or films) should be italicized.

  - Names of shorter works (articles or chapters) should be placed in double quotation marks.

- As was stated before, quotations from prose that take more than five lines should be blocked (for an example look at the "General Chicago/Turabian Style Features" section above).

References

- In Chicago/Turabian style they are compiled in a section titled "Bibliography." This title is placed on a separate page and centered on the top.

- Two empty lines must be placed between the title and the first entry.

- Entries are separated from each other by one empty line space.

- All entries are listed in alphabetical order.

- If a source has more than one author, "and" (not "&") is used for their listing.

  → If a source has two or three authors, all of them have to be presented.

  → If a source has four and more authors, all of them have to be listed in the bibliography. However, in notes, write only the first author and then add "et al."

  → If an author is unknown, mention it by its title in the text, notes, and bibliography.

  → Publishers' names must be written in full.

  → Publication dates should be written only if they are known.

  → The abbreviation "n.d." is used for print works of which the publication date is uncertain.

  → If you use an Internet source, give its URL/DOI.

  → It is also acceptable to mention the volume (vol.), equation (eq.), or section (sec.) of a source.

The Notes-Bibliography (NB) in More Details

The system consists of notes (footnotes and endnotes) that have to be used every time a particular source is mentioned in writing, no matter whether an author incorporates a direct quote or paraphrases it.

Footnotes are normally placed at the end of the page where sources were used. Endnotes, in their turn, finish a chapter or the whole document. In general terms, a superscript number which is relevant to a certain footnote is applied at the end of the sentence or clause which contains a reference to a source. A corresponding note with detailed bibliographic information concerning it is placed at the bottom of the page.

Look at the example below:

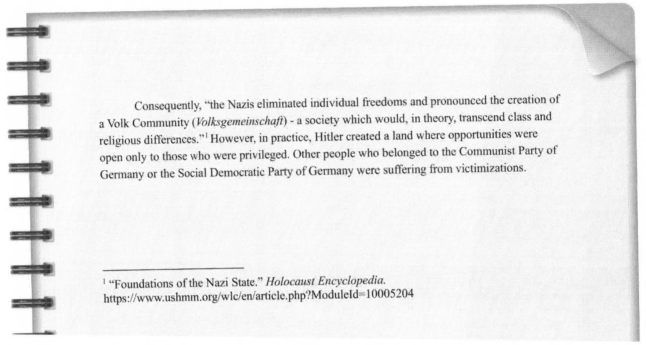

Consequently, "the Nazis eliminated individual freedoms and pronounced the creation of a Volk Community (*Volksgemeinschaft*) - a society which would, in theory, transcend class and religious differences."[1] However, in practice, Hitler created a land where opportunities were open only to those who were privileged. Other people who belonged to the Communist Party of Germany or the Social Democratic Party of Germany were suffering from victimizations.

[1] "Foundations of the Nazi State." *Holocaust Encyclopedia.* https://www.ushmm.org/wlc/en/article.php?ModuleId=10005204

As you can see from the example, the number of a note is placed after the quotation marks are closed and the citation is finished. A footnote itself begins below after the same superscript number.

It is important to note that the first footnote contains all relevant information concerning the source:

- The author's name.
- The title of the source.
- Information about its publication.

More notes for one source must incorporate only the last name of the author, shortened title of the source (if initially it has more than four words), and the page number.

If one source is used more than two times, a relevant note must contain the word "Ibid." which means "in the same place."

If you use different pages from one particular source, incorporate "Ibid." in the corresponding note. This useful word then is followed by the new number of the page.

In-Text Citations and References

As was stated before, citations are marked by footnotes. When the very first citation ends, a superscribed number "1" is placed after it. Important features are as follows:

1. Numbers are always placed at the end of a sentence, clause with quotation, or paraphrasing of the material from the source.

2. The first footnote is indented half an inch from the left side of the page.

3. Others footnotes should be flushed to the left.

4. Place a bold line between each footnote.

5. If special commentary is needed, write it after the actual information concerning the footnote is given. Separate the commentary from the footnote by a period.

Look at the example below:

Hitler's wish to conquer the whole world was strong. Researchers admit also that he invented "the Führer principle."[1] By it "authority - in government, the party, economy, family, and so on - flowed downward and was to be obeyed unquestioningly."[2] It is quite to assume that not all people who were close to the dreadful ruler shared his ideas. Obviously, Hitler was obsessed with a regime. It is also a common knowledge that he was insane. However, there are doctors, who admit that he was mentally healthy and understood all actions that he did.[3] However, it is evident that other Germans had no opportunity even to think about this Hitler's misdoings.

---

[1] "Foundations of the Nazi State." *Holocaust Encyclopedia.* https://www.ushmm.org/wlc/en/article.php?ModuleId=10005204
[2] "Foundations of the Nazi State." *Holocaust Encyclopedia.* https://www.ushmm.org/wlc/en/article.php?ModuleId=10005204
[3] Sherratt, Yvonne. "Was Hitler Ill? A Final Diagnosis." Times Higher Education. Last modified December 13, 2012. https://www.timeshighereducation.com/books/book-reviews/was-hitler-ill-a-final-diagnosis/422091.article

How to Cite Books

Footnote/endnote (N): 1) Firstname Lastname, *Title of Book* (Place of publication: Publisher, Year of publication), page number.

Bibliographical entry (B): Last name, First name. *Title of Book.* Place of publication: Publisher, year of publication.

A Book That Is Written by One Author

N: 2) Sean Taylor, *Silly Things I Tell to My Wife* (Los Angeles: The Family Publisher, 2017), 34.

B: Taylor, Sean. *Silly Things I Tell to My Wife.* Los Angeles: The Family Publisher, 2017.

A Book That Is Written by Several Authors

N: 3). Sean Taylor and Kelly Young, *American Classical Movies in Modern Interpretation* (Los Angeles: UCLA, 2016), 45-89

B: Taylor, Sean, and Young, Kelly. *American Classical Movies in Modern Interpretation.* Los Angeles: UCLA, 2016.

A Translated Work (Written by One Author)

N: 4). Alexander Pushkin, *Eugene Onegin*, trans. Charles Hepburn Johnston (New York: Russian Into English, 1957), 123.

B: Pushkin, Alexander. *Eugene Onegin.* Translated by Charles Hepburn Johnston. New York: Russian Into English, 1957.

A Book with Author and Editor

N: 5). Sean A. Taylor, *Story of My Traveling to My Love*, ed. Kelly Young (San Diego: San Diego City College, 2017), 44.

B: Taylor, Sean A. *Story of My Traveling to My Love,* Edited by Kelly Young. San Diego: San Diego City College, 2017.

An Article, Essay, Short Story, Chapter in an Edition

N: 6). Bernard Chilson, "The Present," in *The Best American Short Stories about Love 1946*, ed. Jeremy Nail (Chicago: The Best Book Publisher, 1946), 89.

B: Chilson, Bernard. "The Present." In *The Best American Short Stories about Love 1946*, edited by Jeremy Nail, 76-102. Chicago: The Best Book Publisher, 1946.

When an Author Is Unknown

Such sources are cited by their titles. The sequence of data concerning the source is similar to the situation when an author is known. State everything else that is known.

When Citing an Indirect Source

This is not recommended in academic writing. However, when it is impossible to find the initial source, follow this rule:

N: 6. Sean Taylor, Be Happy, Be Silly (Cambridge, MA: Harvard University Press, 2000), 24, quoted in Kelly Young, Letters for My Kids (Los Angeles: Inspiring Writing, 2017), 78.

How to Cite Periodicals

Journals

For print journals: Author's name, Article Title, Journal Title, and issue information (volume, issue number, month, year, page numbers).

N: 1. Sean Taylor, "Letters to My Wife," *Be Happy and Prosper* 23, no. 4 (2017): 78.

B: Taylor, Sean. "Letters to My Wife." *Be Happy and Prosper* 23, no. 4 (2017): 60-84.

For online journals also include retrieval data, date of access, and DOI/URL.

N: 1. Sean Taylor, "Letters to My Wife," *Be Happy and Prosper* 23, no. 4 (2017): 78, accessed September 13, 2017, http:// the name of the site (the electronic address which can lead to the journal).

B: Taylor, Sean. "Letters to My Wife." *Be Happy and Prosper* 23, no. 4 (2017): 60-84. Accessed September 13, 2017. http:// the name of the site (the electronic address which can lead to the journal).

Magazines

Author's name, the title of an article, the title of a magazine, date.

N: 1. Sean Taylor, "Letters to My Wife," *Happiness Magazine,* September 2017, 44.

B: Taylor, Sean. "Letters to My Wife." *Happiness Magazine,* September 2017.

Online Magazines

The same information as about print magazines and also DOI/URL.

N: 1. Kelly Young, The Night Before, *Family,* February 4, 2017, http:// the name of the site (the electronic address which can lead to the journal).

B: Young, Kelly. The Night Before, *Family,* February 4, 2017. http:// the name of the site (the electronic address which can lead to the journal).

Newspapers

Author's name, column heading, the name of a newspaper, month (abbreviated), day, year. A page number may be not stated if an issue takes more than one edition. If a newspaper is online, URL/DOI should be presented.

N: 1. Kelly Young, "The Night Before," *Family*, (Huntington Beach, CA), Feb. 4, 2017.

B: Young, Kelly. "The Night Before." *Family*, (Huntington Beach, CA), Feb. 4, 2017.

How to Cite Web Sources

A general citing looks like that:

N: 1. Firstname Lastname, "Title of a Web Page," *An Italicized Name of a Website,* publication date/access date, URL.

B: Lastname, Firstname. "Title of a Web Page." *An Italicized Name of a Website,* publication date/access date, URL.

How to Cite Films, TV Shows, Other Recorded Media Products

A general citing of these sources looks like the following:

N: 1. Firstname Lastname, *Title of Source.* Format, performed/directed by Firstname Lastname (An initial year of release; City: Distributor/Studio, Video release year.), Medium.

B: Lastname, Firstname. *Title of Source.* Format, performed/directed by Firstname Lastname. An initial year of release. City: Distributor/Studio, Video release year. Medium.

All in all, Chicago/Turabian style seems to be more complicated than MLA style in academic writing. It has more peculiarities that need to be accounted for. However, in actual practice, the most attention should be paid to footnotes and endnotes and the bibliography. Our complete guide presents full information concerning these issues. Refer to it for the successful writing of your assignments.

Work Cited

Purdue Online Writing Web. "Chicago Manual of Style 16th Edition." Purdue OWL. *purdue.edu,* owl.english.purdue.edu/owl/resource/717/01/. Accessed 13 Sept. 2017.

4.4. Harvard Formatting Style

Harvard style of essay writing is used for creating academic works for many scholarly subjects. It is most common in institutions of learning in the United Kingdom and Australia. Harvard style is based on an author-date system of references. Also, it has stable norms which still can vary a little bit regarding punctuation, abbreviation, italicization, and capitalization.

An author-date system implies that in-text citations include the name of the author and year when the work was published. However, if a citation is taken from an exact work, it is advisable to mention the page number of this quote.

> *The most common sickness that is related to sugar comes down to tooth decay. As researchers admit, it "is caused by the acid made by bacteria that grow in sugar. The acid eats away at the enamel of the teeth"* (***Kid's Health, 2015, p.134***).

If you summarize or paraphrase a quotation from a particular author's work, a page number must also be mentioned.

> *Lactose represents another type of sugar. It can be found in dairy foods. What is more, there is fructose that is stored in fruits* (***Mundasad, 2014, p.89***).

More information concerning in-text citations will be presented further.

A Cover Page in Harvard Style

Work that is written in Harvard style has a separate cover page. The name of the paper is written in capital letters a third of the way down the page. The name of the author of the paper is placed about three lines below, and is typed in regular letters. About four lines down, there is the name of the class and the name of the professor. Then, the name of school, city or state, and the date.

Look at the example below:

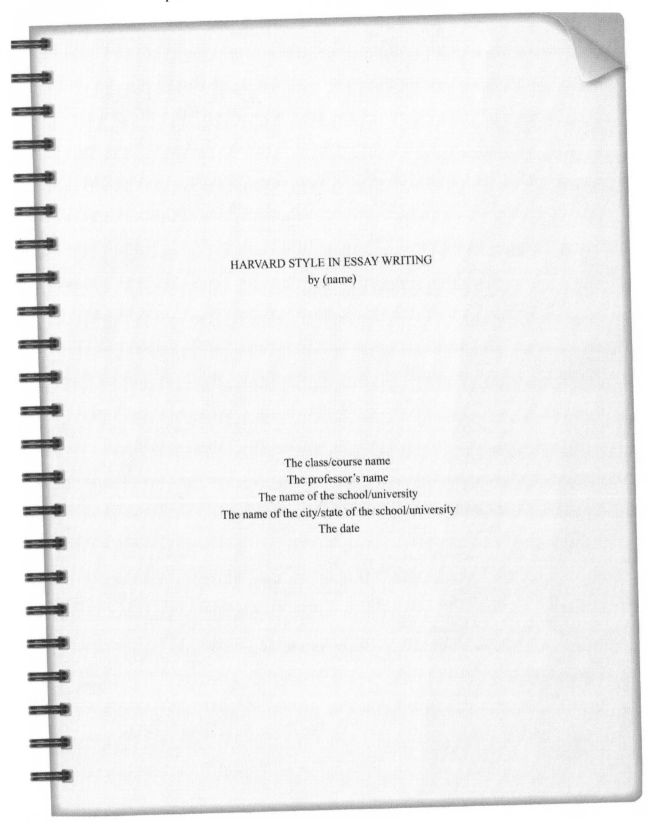

HARVARD STYLE IN ESSAY WRITING
by (name)

The class/course name
The professor's name
The name of the school/university
The name of the city/state of the school/university
The date

Header

In Harvard style, it is necessary to use a header on every page of work. It consists of a shortened title and relevant page number. For example, if an essay is named as "American Romantic Poetry of the 19th Century," a short description of the title will be "Romantic Poetry of the 19th Century." Specifically, it has to represent the main idea of the paper (the central focus of it). Such a phrase is placed on the right side of a header line:

Romantic Poetry of the 19th Century   1

There are five spaces between the name of the header and the page number.

Academic works created in Harvard Style are normally typed with the help of a standard in Times New Roman font. It is also possible to use Arial, Times, Helvetica, or Courier New. All in all, a text must be easy to interpret, so it is better to type it in a 12 point size. No fancy fonts, colorful words, underlining, or useless italics and bold should be used. The whole text should be double-spaced with regular left and right margins.

All names of large works such as books, films, newspapers, TV shows, plays, websites, and magazines are italicized. Titles of shorter sources are put in quotation marks.

In-Text Citations and References

As was stated before, Harvard style implies the author-date referencing. When a quotation demands mention of two authors, their names appear in parentheses in alphabetical order.

For example: (Taylor 2016; Young 2015).

If there are more than two authors, their names must be listed in the order in which they occur on the title page.

For example: (Taylor, Young & Jemmerson 2004).

If a quotation contains more than thirty words, it should be placed in a special block. In such a way, it can be typed in a smaller font and indented from the left margin. Leave a blank line before a quotation and after it. Type it in single-spaced format. Its separation from the initial text should be visible. For example:

> It was found that:
>
> Neurons that allow this vital tissue to be fully operative begin to misfire and engage in a haphazard activity. This action usually creates a scatterbrain effect. There are many resulting symptoms to metabolic brain dysfunction, most notably attention deficit disorder and its related ailments (Clement 2012, p.45).

The table below provides examples of common sources for referencing and formats of their citations.

Name of Source	In-Text Citation	Relevant Reference
A book (1 author)	Taylor (2016)/(Taylor 2016)	Taylor, SA 2016, *American movies in modern perspective*, UCLA, Los Angeles, California.
A book (2-3 authors)	(Taylor, Young & Jemmerson 2016)	Taylor, SA, Young, KL & Jemmerson, TY 2016, *Sugar Consumption*, San Diego, California.
A book (more than three authors)	(Taylor et al. 2016)	Taylor, SA, Young, KL & Jemmerson, TY & Fancy, RP 2016, *Better opportunities in small business*, San-Francisco, California.
A book (with unknown author)	(Poems in despair 2003)	*Poems in despair*, 2003, Irwin, Sydney.
A book (with editor)	(Grant 2005)	Grant, CW (ed) 2005, *Business in Australia*, Academic Press, New York.
A book (with more than one editor)	(Grant & Bergman 2007)	Grant, CW & Bergman, IH (eds) 2007, *How to build your career*, Best Editions, London.
A book (chapter/article from it)	(Taylor 2015, p.67)	Taylor, SA 2015, '*A writer grows from line to line*' in K Young & C Bergman, (eds), Poetry rules and recommendations, p.58-72, Macmillan Press, London

A book (different works by the same author written in one year)	(Taylor 2016a) (Taylor 2016b)	Taylor, SA 2016a, *Movie ethics*, UCLA, Los Angeles, California. Taylor SA 2016b, *Camera angles in Hitchcock movies*, San Diego, California.
Dictionary/Encyclopedia	In the Encyclopedia Britannica (2016) it is stated that...	Does not need to be included in a reference list.
A journal article (printed)	(Taylor & Young 1997)	Taylor, SA & Young, KG 1997, 'Art-therapy', *Healthy Children*, vol.45, no.8, pp.45-78.
A journal article (electronic)	(Masyr 2013)	Masyr, B 2013, 'Be confident and prosper', *Leadership* Advice, vol.34, no.3, pp.89-100.
A journal article (online, no volume, number, pages)	(Hackley & Reverene 2011)	Hackley, M & Reverene,C 2011, 'Tension', *American Journal for Immigrants*. Available from http:// the URL of the website where the article can be found.

A website
 	
*** features that have to be included:*
 	
  • *The author of the site.*
  • *The date the site was created/last updated.*
  • *Name of the company on which platform the site was*
	(University Library 2010)	University Library 2010, *University Library Home page*, 15 September 2017, University of California, Los Angeles. Available from http:// the URL of the University website.

created/sponsor. • *URL.* • *Date of viewing of the site.*		
A web page	(Taylor & Young 2017)	Taylor, SA & Young, KL 2017, *Being a good student*. Available from http:// the URL of the web page. [15 September 2017].
A blog	(Timm 2016)	Timm, M 2015, 'A new style for teenagers', *As Morgan Says*, blog post, 3 June. Available from http:// the URL of the blog. [15 September 2017].
Facebook	(Law of Attraction 2015)	Law of Attraction 2015, *How to manifest all your desires*, Facebook post, 23 March. Available from http:// the URL of the post. [15 September 2017].
Youtube	(TED Talks 2011)	TED Talks 2011, *Sean Taylor: Letters to my beloved wife*, Youtube video, 4 February. Available from http:// the URL of the video. [15 September 2017].
Newspaper (printed)	(Barkley 2016)	Barkley, J 2016, 'How to build your self-esteem', *The American,* 10 October, p. 4.

Newspaper (electronic)	(Barkley 2016)	Barkley, J 2016, 'How to build your self-esteem', *The American,* 10 October, p. 4. Available from: Success. [15 September 2017].
Newspaper (from a website)	(Barkley 2016)	Barkley, J 2016, 'How to build your self-esteem', *The American,* 10 October, p. 4. Available from: www. The name of the website. [15 September 2017].
Newspaper (with no author)	('How to build your self-esteem' 2016)	*'How to build your self-esteem'* 2016, New York Times, 10 May, p.8.
When citing information that was cited by someone else	(Taylor, cited in Young 2009)	Young, K 2009, 'How to build a monetized Instagram account', *The Australian Journal*, vol.45 no.7, pp.98-100.

Harvard style is another format for academic papers that has its peculiarities. They all have to be thoroughly studied before the process of writing begins. Our detailed guide proposes visual material, and with the help of this material, creating academic works in Harvard style will be easy.

Works Cited

The University of Australia. "Harvard Citation Style: Introduction." *uwa.edu.au,*
    guides.library.uwa.edu.au/c.php?g=380288&p=2575698. Accessed 15 Sept. 2017.

Uvocorp. "Harvard Formatting and Style Guide." uvocorp.com/dl/Harvard%20Guide.pdf. Accessed
    15 Sept. 2017.

Chapter 5. Development of Academic Writing Skills

Academic writing is a type of narration that is considered conventional in scholarly society. For this reason, people who face it for the first time may find it complicated and diverse. Like any activity, academic writing requires a particular set of skills. These skills can be developed through the practice of special exercises and the learning of certain tips which make writing easier.

This chapter of our guide focuses on important features of academic narration and presents practical activities that help every writer to understand nuances of scholarly composition better. Further, you will find out:

- Why **focus and clarity** are the leading characteristics of academic writing.
- Which **voice** (direct, indirect, paraphrasing, summarizing) is better in which occasion.
- Why **reflective writing** applies to any academic essay and which issues can be solved with its help.
- How to **reflect correctly** and not be afraid of your personal view even in research papers.
- Which **words help to connect ideas** for particular purposes (such as for *emphasizing, adding information, comparison, generalization, contrasting*, and others).
- Which questions will help you to check whether **your work is original** or not.
- How to **add originality** even to academic work that should refer to other scholarly sources.

Also, you will be given **exercises** with the help of which you can learn how to:

122

- **Paraphrase correctly** with different methods of paraphrasing.

- **Summarize correctly**.

- **Map out ideas** for your writing in order to determine central points and avoid missing anything.

Refer to our complete guide to learn how to develop academic writing skills and be more confident concerning your studies. Following tips and exercises provides insight into the scholarly type of narration so that your writing becomes better and clearer.

Developing Academic Writing Skills – Tips and Exercises

Academic writing has its peculiarities. In order to develop great skills that will help to complete school assignments quickly and easily, pay attention to the aspects that are presented in this chapter of our guide.

Focus and Clarity

The main characteristic of academic writing boils down to clarity. Research papers of all kinds refer to a great variety of people. They should be comprehensible to all members of academic, and sometimes non-academic, society. What is more, a precise narration allows the reader's attention to focus on the facts that are presented, and not on linguistic aspects that tell about these facts. Academic style is always focused and direct.

For making your academic writing clear, follow the steps below:

- **Start each paragraph with a topic sentence.** It has to express the main idea of a section that is to begin. The next sentences should present a detailed explanation of the topic statement.

  People do not experience miracles in their lives because they do not believe in them. It is easier for humans to be afraid and choose something comfortable and familiar. How many people stay faithful to themselves and follow their dreams? You can count them throughout historical periods since the majority of them became famous for changes they made. All great people are special with their courage, vision, and faith. When we talk about their accomplishments, we think that they were lucky to do what they did. We forget that they were also hardworking, passionate, and persistent. They experienced miracles which came from their efforts, beliefs, and the complete confidence that everything is possible.

In this example, the first sentence makes a claim concerning the presence of miracles in people's lives. The following sentences give supportive evidence that shows why the statement is true.

- **The central topic of a paragraph may be given in the form of a subject at the beginning of the topic sentence.** It helps to focus the reader's attention on a point of interest easily. Try not to overwhelm the first sentence of a paragraph with useless words so your central topic will not get lost among them. Compare two topic sentences:

  - *The great American film critic and scriptwriter who ... was Kevin Jefferson.*
  - *Kevin Jefferson was an American film critic and scriptwriter ...*

The second example is better since it reveals the main focus of a discussion right away.

- **Go from old to new facts.** This is especially useful for avoiding repetition and making a narration coherent.

  Kevin Jefferson *was most famous for his articles about Hitchcock movies.* ***His*** *unforgettable peculiarity that was loved by many readers boils down to his humor.* ***The critic*** *was very generous for funny statements and remarks.* ***Jefferson*** *could observe every movie as something totally silly. Despite the fact that Hitchcock made dozens of serious dramatic films that easily frightened viewers,* ***the critic*** *wrote about them in such a radiant way that even haters became interested in psychological thrillers.*

In this example, we see how old information brings new facts. Each sentence provides new details concerning the main character of the paragraph. Readers can easily gain knowledge from this writing without losing the central idea or being trapped in too many useless words.

- **Move from easy facts to more complicated ones.** It means that the most detailed information should be moved to the end of a paragraph. Again, do not overload the beginning with excessive words since they complicate a perception. Compare two examples:

  1. Twenty-four articles, forty reviews, fifty-nine comments, and several proposals stand alongside some scripts in his creative heritage.

  2. His famous critical works, including a number of scripts, consist of twenty-four articles, forty reviews, fifty-nine comments, and several proposals.

The second sentence is easier than the first one so readers will find it more comfortable.

- **Give more important information at the end of a sentence**. A peculiarity of human perception is that people always better remember statements that begin a conversation and end it. Conclude your writing with facts that you want your readers to keep in mind long after the reading will be finished.

- **Emphasize the most important issues and de-emphasize the less significant ones** by incorporating single main points in short separate sentences.

- **Repeat information from previous sentences before giving new details.**

   *His unforgettable peculiarity that was loved by many readers boils down to his humor. **The critic** was very generous for funny statements and remarks.*

   The words "The critic" refers to "His" which was used in the previous sentence. Both mentions touch upon one person who is discussed in the paragraph.

Voice in Academic Writing

Academic voice defines the expression of the writer's thoughts. Specifically, it can belong to a writer personally or it can summarize or paraphrase someone else's words. It is important to use both these manners of speaking since academic writing demands references to other sources as well as a personal understanding of them.

A personal voice helps to build a scholarly argument while a referential voice introduces a valid support to it. Sometimes, it is also significant to give opposite statements to your ideas so that readers can think which positions are right.

There are several ways to include referential voice into your writing:

- **Direct and indirect voice.**

Direct voice represents your personal ideas or original quotations from people you refer to. Such citations always strengthen your argument since they point to someone else that shares your claim.

   *As historical records state, Luther gained his spiritual concern after an accident he experienced. He appeared to be in the center of a thunderstorm and was so afraid that he referred to a prayer. Luther promised to become a monk if he remained alive. As we see, he completed his promise. **According to researchers, "The Augustinian Hermits which Luther joined was founded in the middle of the thirteenth century as a mendicant order — that is, the Augustinian monks depended upon begging for their livelihood" (Waibel 2).***

Do not forget that in many academic styles, quotations that have more than 30 words should be put into a block and separated from the initial text.

- **Paraphrasing or summarizing.**

This technique is used to make general statements concerning someone else's ideas. *Paraphrasing* boils down to narrating information from another source in your own words. It is important to maintain the main idea of the author clearly while transforming the text where it was given. Paraphrasing generally takes the same volume as the original text. *Summarizing*, in its turn, is shorter and presents only the most significant points of the initial source. It demands the writer to demonstrate an understanding of what is important for stating and what is not. In such a way, summarizing allows a writer to incorporate his personal voice in writing.

> *Paraphrase*: As a result, he fulfilled his promise and delved into the religion for the first time in his life (Waibel 2).

> *Summary*: He delved into the religion for the first time (Waibel 2).

How to Paraphrase Correctly

- Read a passage first and try to understand it as a whole unit. Do not split it into separate ideas; grab a general meaning instead.

- Do not paraphrase each sentence of the passage. Choose some main points and transform them into your own writing.

- Use your own words. However, be precise about the meaning. Do not misrepresent your personal understanding as someone else's words. Paraphrase first and then add your view.

- Use original quotations and phrases where they are needed. Do not forget to place them into quotation marks.

Methods of Paraphrasing

1. Read a source and then write.

> If you prefer to be as independent in your writing as possible, focus on your personal understanding of the author's statements. Again, be sure that you give the understanding of the words of others and not your own meaning of things. When you paraphrase, you restate. When you add your ideas, you create. All in all, read a source to its full apprehension and then move to writing.

2. Make notes.

Note down exact ideas from a source while reading. Then paraphrase them by:

- Changing the structure of sentences.

- Changing words.

How to Summarize Correctly

Follow the strategies below if you are not confident in your summarizing skills:

1. Read text carefully.

2. What is its purpose?

- What is the author trying to tell by his writing?
- What aim do you pursue while making a summary of this source?
- Did you create a summary for making your arguments strong?
- Did you create a summary for criticizing the source so your writing can prove a different point of view?

3. Choose the major points from the source:

- Look for them in topic sentences.
- Distinguish the main information from secondary facts.
- Avoid large examples, details, and illustrations.
- Pick up different words for the summary but leave specific vocabulary (terms and key concepts).

4. Transform the structure of the source. Change its grammar (rearrange the sequence of nouns, verbs, adverbs, adjectives). Divide long sentences into small ones and combine initially short into larger units.

5. Use words such as *however, since, although,* and *therefore* between sentences.

6. Check your summary by being sure that:

- Your goal of the summary is clearly presented.
- The meaning of your writing is the same as it was in the initial text.
- The summary is done in your own style.

Mapping Out Ideas

This exercise allows you to create a visual representation of arguments you want to present in writing. It helps with:

- Clarifying connections between ideas.
- Connecting new concepts with those that are present already.
- Organizing all ideas in a logical order.

As we remember, any academic writing includes references from valid sources. On their basis, students make their concepts. Specifically, new ideas on a particular subject of interest come from already stated issues. In order to make clear arguments that need to be addressed in a new essay, map them out. Follow hints below to simplify this process:

- Carefully read the source(s) that related to the subject of your writing.

- Note down main arguments of authors.

- Build the connection between them.

- What can you personally add to these arguments?

- What is your attitude toward them (supportive or objective)?

- What can be taken as an illustration to all arguments? Pick up some great quotes that will provide more information to readers.

Maps of ideas are usually very dynamic. They can grow bigger and become quite endless when a writer gets more information concerning a subject. However, it is important to organize arguments logically and move from the major ideas to secondary ones. Pay attention to instructions that professors always give. In them, they highlight main aspects that have to be addressed in an essay. Organize your map around them and do not move forward if it is unnecessary. Always remember that the more statements you give, the better knowledge concerning them you need to provide.

For an example of a concept map look below:

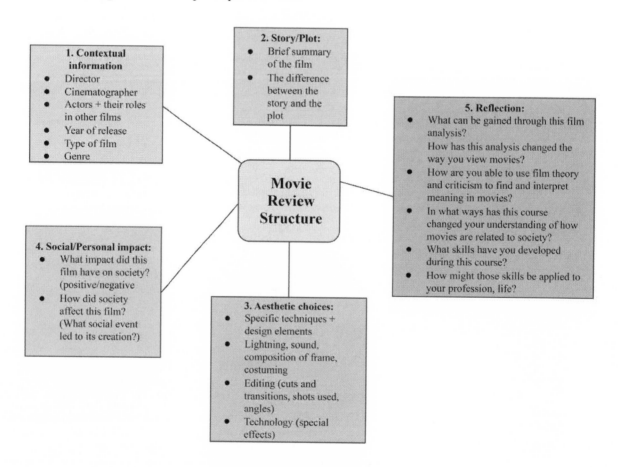

This concept map includes all aspects that have to be addressed for a good movie review. It will help a student not to miss something and organize the narration in the logical order.

Reflective Writing

Reflective writing implies that an author analyzes some experience or event that has already happened and states perspectives to it.

Reflective writing works through reconsidering experiences concerning a subject of interest. It is usually applied to medicine, sociology, psychology, and other disciplines that deal both with theories and their practical implementation. Through reflective writing, a student can question causes of things, evaluate situations in which they occur, and apply critical thinking for creating solutions. In such a way, this type of narration demands a strong personal voice from the writer. A particular problem has to be solved and an essay represents how its author will do this. Reflective writing is more subjective, as it does not demand extensive reliance on valid sources. A student can freely use "I" in order to critically evaluate information concerning a subject and relations between theory and practice.

Reflective writing can be carefully incorporated in part in almost any academic paper. It is not only about usage of personal pronouns but concerning why things are the way they are, why they work as they do, and why we evaluate their work in this (positive/negative) manner.

Here is an example of reflective writing:

> *Researchers admit that sleep deprivation slows time of reaction, decreases memory abilities, and disturbs the normal learning process (Chee & Chaa, 2003). In order to check these findings in practice, we made an experiment in our class. Specifically, we tested how self-reported sleep deprivation on the night before the trial appeared to be connected with false memories of watching a particular sudden event.*

Connecting Ideas in Writing

The best way to connect ideas is to use special words. Some of them are presented below:

Purpose	Examples
To add an idea	also, and, as well (as), further, moreover, furthermore, additionally, too, apart from this, in addition, what is more
To estimate a condition	unless, if, provided that, unless

To compare similar things	in a similar manner, equally, similarly, for the same reason, in comparison, one the one hand, correspondingly, too
To contrast opposite things	although, yet, whereas, despite, even, in spite of, while, but, rather, nevertheless, on the other hand, conversely, however, nonetheless, still, instead, in contrast, still, alternatively, though
To emphasize	in fact, most importantly, indeed, unquestionably, it should be noted that, again, to repeat
To illustrate	for example, for instance, as follows, thus, such as
To restate	in other words, namely, that is, another way, put it differently, specifically
To show cause-effect relations	due to, because of, the result of, since, as a consequence
To show an effect of something	consequently, as a result, hence, for this reason, thus, therefore, so, accordingly
To show concession	although, however, admittedly, obviously, indeed, even though
To generalize	generally, in general, usually, in most cases, as a rule, on the whole, for the most part
To show a sequence	firstly, secondly, next, finally, meanwhile, while, then, subsequently, later, to conclude

How to Develop Originality

The concept of originality means that a student has to avoid plagiarism and provide a good understanding of his writing. There is no need to make an academic writing too creative. The point is that every writer has his personal perception of any subject. Even when two students read the same

130

source, there is a chance that they use different quotations from it. They both develop diverse subjective attitudes to material which will be later incorporated into an academic work.

Originality also means a careful use of words, phrases, and other notions that are used in an essay. What is more, it comes down to:

- Creating a new product or improving one that is present.
- Analyzing a theory from a new point of view.
- Testing someone's idea.
- Working on some product that was not finished before.
- Providing detailed research for some questionable product.
- Applying a new or unusual approach to some product.
- Giving a different interpretation of existing information.
- Applying existing research on a different basis.
- Applying existing concepts to different areas.
- Developing new research.
- Making a study in a new area.
- Researching a subject that was never studied before.
- Analyzing results of a study concerning a particular subject.

If a student does something from the list above in the essay, it means that his work is original. A good academic essay needs to address all of the mentioned aspects. Use them in your writing to make it coherent, smooth, valid, and scientific.

Works Cited

The University of Melbourne. "Concept Mapping." *unimelb.edu.au,* library.unimelb.edu.au/__data/assets/pdf_file/0010/1924066/Concept_Mapping.pdf. Accessed 19 Sept. 2017.

The University of Melbourne. "Connecting Ideas in Writing." *unimelb.edu.au,* services.unimelb.edu.au/__data/assets/pdf_file/0019/532900/Connecting-ideas-in-academic-writing-Update-030816.pdf. Accessed 19 Sept. 2017.

The University of Melbourne. "Developing Clarity and Focus in Academic Writing." *unimelb.edu.au,* services.unimelb.edu.au/__data/assets/pdf_file/0006/471291/Developing_clarity_ and_focus_Update_051112.pdf. Accessed 19 Sept. 2017.

The University of Melbourne. "Developing Originality." *unimelb.edu.au,* services.unimelb.edu.au/__data/assets/pdf_file/0009/471267/Developing_originality_Update_051112.pdf. Accessed 19 Sept. 2017.

The University of Melbourne. "Voice in Academic Writing." *unimelb.edu.au,* services.unimelb.edu.au/__data/assets/pdf_file/0004/471298/Voice_in_Academic_Writing_Update_051112.pdf. Accessed 20 Sept. 2017.

The University of Melbourne. "Writing Reflectively." *unimelb.edu.au,* services.unimelb.edu.au/__data/assets/pdf_file/0011/675776/Writing_Reflectively_051112.pdf. Accessed 19 Sept. 2017.

The University of Wisconsin – Madison. "How to Paraphrase a Source." *Writing Center,* writing.wisc.edu/Handbook/QPA_paraphrase2.html. Accessed 19 Sept. 2017.

Using English for Academic Purposes for Students in Higher Education. "Summarising & Note-Taking." *uefap.com,* uefap.com/reading/notetake/summary.htm. Accessed 19 Sept. 2017.

Final Thoughts

Bidding farewell is always sad, so how wonderful it is that we don't need to do it. *Move the Rock of Academic Writing* will be a good assistant for you throughout the entire educational process because even the most skilled aces have to return to studying the nuts and bolts every now and then. Keep this book close to you and get back to it as soon as you need assistance.

Move the Rock of Academic Writing is not the first in the EssayShark series. Read our other books to learn about different types of essays and letters. Also, *Move the Rock of Academic Writing* is not the last. Soon, you'll be able to get acquainted with the fifth book. Let the inspiration and writing spirit be with you and good luck with achieving all your academic goals!

Made in the USA
Middletown, DE
21 June 2020